The Mysterious Tramp

Nadakkavu, Kozhikode, Kerala, 673011
www.insightpublica.com
e-mail: insightpublica@gmail.com

Title: **THE MYSTERIOUS TRAMP**
Author: **VERE C. BARCLAY**
First Insight Edition: July 2024
Copyright © Reserved
All rights reserved.
Printed and Published by
InsightinPublica Printers & Publishers Pvt. Ltd.
ISBN 9789355175830

The Mysterious Tramp

Vera C. Barclay

Vera C. Barclay

(10 November 1893 - 19 September 1989)

Vera Charlesworth Barclay co-founder of Cubs 1916, was an English pioneer of Scouting and an author. She was an early exponent of female leadership in the Scout movement and played a leading role in the introduction of the Wolf Cub programme for younger boys, both in the United Kingdom and in France

"The Mysterious Tramp" by Vera C. Barclay is a classic children's novel that tells the story of a young boy named Peter who encounters a mysterious tramp in his neighborhood. The tramp, who is kind and wise, becomes a friend to Peter and teaches him valuable life lessons about kindness, courage, and the importance of helping others. As Peter navigates the challenges of growing up, the tramp's guidance helps him to develop into a thoughtful and compassionate individual. This heartwarming tale is a delightful read for both children and adults alike.

Contents

CHAPTER I

BY FIRELIGHT

The night nursery was in darkness, save for the red glow of the fire, and the occasional flickering light of a little yellow flame that seemed to wake up every now and then and light up the room, casting strange black shadows on the ceiling. In three little white beds lay three boys. At least they should have been lying, but, as a matter of fact, two were sitting up, with expressions of sullen rage upon their tear-stained faces, and one was lying in a huddled heap beneath the bedclothes, sobbing.

"For goodness' sake stop that beastly sniveling, you little cry-baby," said David.

The sobbing ceased for a minute, then, from beneath the bedclothes, came the muffled voice of Nipper. "I—I'm not a cry-cry-cry baby." The sobbing went on.

"Nipper," said David sternly, "you have no reason to bleat like that. You only got four, an me and Bill got a dozen each."

This brought Nipper from beneath the bedclothes.

"That's 'cos I have more sense in my little finger than you two fat-heads have in the whole of your bodies. I trod hard on grandfather's worst corn, and that made him drop the birch. I jolly soon picked it up, and threw it out of the window. And he couldn't find nothing else to beat me with, so he let me go. It's not for the beating I'm crying, it's for something else. I was going to tell you about it, but as you're both such beasts I shan't now."

Having delivered himself of this speech, Nipper retired under the bedclothes, and began a series of mournful sounds. Now, though David was ready of speech and full of ideas, Bill, his twin, was a man of action. It was always David who thought of splendid schemes, but Bill who carried them out. Leaning far out of his bed he reached for one of his boots, and, taking a careful aim, landed it with a thud upon Nipper's huddled figure. This brought forth Nipper's own special performance and chief means of defence, a siren-like shriek. As was to be expected, it brought Nurse to the door.

"Now then, you naughty boys," she said, "if I hear another sound I shall go and tell your gran'pa."

"You can jolly well go," said David, "he's lost the birch."

"If you aren't quiet at once," continued Nurse, "I shall not allow you to go to the horseshow to-morrow."

"That's all right," said David. "Grandfather has already forbidden us to go——"

"But we're jolly well going all the same," added Bill in an aside.

"You shan't have any jam for breakfast," said poor old Nurse in despair. This was a serious matter.

"Then here goes," said Bill, in a spasm of rage, and he let fly his remaining boot.

It struck the old Nurse very hard on the hand. She had rheumatism, and the blow hurt her. With a little exclamation of pain she retired, and shut the door.

A regular bally-rag then began. Pillows flew across the room, and before the fight was finished Bill's nightshirt was torn from top to bottom, and David's nose was bleeding.

And in the playroom Nurse was talking sadly to Eliza as she darned the boys' stockings. The piece of news she was giving Eliza was the very piece of news that Nipper had heard, and which had caused his tears.

"The master has given me notice," she said, wiping her

eyes. "He says it's all my fault the way the boys behave, and it's got so terrible he won't stand it a moment longer. He's given me notice, and he's going to get a strict governess, who won't stand any nonsense, and will get them into good discipline. From the day those twins were born I've looked after them—ten years, now. And Nipper's just on eight—and I've got to leave them!" Poor old Nurse laid her head down on the basket of stockings and broke down. Since the boys' parents had been drowned in a shipwreck the old woman had had them under her care, but they had repaid her with selfishness and disobedience.

The way the "young gentlemen up at the Hall" behaved was the talk of the village. They would steal fruit, not only from their grandfather's glasshouses, but from the poor people's little gardens. They would let out Farmer Johnson's pigs, and chase them all over the village. There was nothing too bad for them to do.

"I pity the person as will have the looking after of them," said Eliza. "I only hope the master will get someone really strict."

CHAPTER II

A COUNCIL OF WAR

It was three weeks later that David called a Council of War in the garden. Nurse had departed with her boxes. Grandfather had engaged a "strict governess."

The Council of War had met in the old pigsty, where all really secret Councils took place. This being a really important Council, the refreshments consisted of peaches and the best hothouse grapes—stolen, of course, from the hothouse, though the boys knew well enough the old gardener would get into trouble with his master, and as likely as not one of the under-gardeners would get the blame.

"And so the dragon is to arrive at six o'clock to-night," said Bill. "Her name is Miss Prince."

"Can't you just see her?" said David, the imaginative one. "She will be very tall and bony, and about a hundred, with grey hair all screwed up in a little knob, and big round goggles, and teeth like an old horse, and a voice like—like—like——"

"Like the ugly sisters in the Cinderella pantomime," said Nipper.

"And she will dress in a stuffy old black dress, all over buttons and spiky whalebone things," added David.

"Well," said Bill, "is war declared?"

"Yes!" shouted the other two.

"And we'll have martial law. Nothing is too bad for Miss Prince," interposed David.

"I say—frightfulness," said Bill.

"Yes—the frightfulest frightfulness," said the other two.

"We will jolly well show her we are not going to be 'managed' or 'disciplined' or bullied," said David.

"We'll bully her," said Bill, "and I bet you she leaves in a week."

"How shall we welcome her?" said David. "I should say an apple-pie bed, with worms and slugs in it."

"Yes. Also mice in her room—they always hate mice."

"And a booby trap on the door."

And so the Council of War proceeded to draw up plans against the new governess.

Meanwhile, a train was speeding along between green fields and leafy woods. In a corner of a carriage sat a girl, looking out of the window, and thinking to herself, "What jolly country for scouting this would be!"

She looked about twenty-four or twenty-five. She had the kind of face a boy would call jolly, and the kind of nice blue eyes that seem to smile at you and make you feel—"This is a friend; one can talk to her and tell her things, and she will understand, although she is a grown-up."

"Well," said Bill, "is war declared?" "Yes," came the determined reply

Presently the girl sighed. "How jolly hard it was saying good-bye to the Cubs!" she thought to herself. "But I mustn't 'give in to myself' and feel unhappy. After all, I am going to some more boys. Dear little chaps, they sound awfully jolly and a good handful to manage. I should feel rather homesick if it was not for the thought of them. But they are sure to give me a good welcome, and we will soon make friends."

She smiled to herself, and the train thundered on between the green fields.

CHAPTER III

THE COMING OF MISS PRINCE

"Listen!" whispered David, "I hear the wheels of the carriage at the front door. Three groans for Miss Prince!"

The front door was opened, and Miss Prince came into the hall. She was just a little disappointed not to see the three boys waiting to welcome her, as she had expected.

"She's not like the Ugly Sisters!" said Nipper in a voice full of disappointment. He was peeping through the balusters, the twins peering over his shoulders.

"I expect that way of smiling and pretending to look nice is just camouflage. She's sure to be a perfect beast inside," said David.

The booby trap unfortunately came down on the housekeeper's head as she showed Miss Prince to her room. The boys distinctly heard Miss Prince laugh, and then pretend she had only coughed and try and comfort Mrs. Biggs. Then they heard her discover the mice in her chest of drawers.

"Mice!" she said. "Dear little things! I love mice. But oh, how cruel! Someone has tied them by their tails!" They heard her freeing the mice. "How untidy my bed looks!" came Miss Prince's voice presently. They heard her open it, then she laughed.

"No go," said Bill dejectedly. "It's going to be harder work giving Miss Prince frightfulness than I thought. But we'll stick to it, won't we, boys?"

"We will!" said the other two.

And they did. Not one civil or friendly word could Miss Prince get from them, try as she would. They were rude to her; they disobeyed her every order; they pretended they could not read at all when she started lessons with them, and added up every sum wrong on purpose. They told her lies, and hid when she wanted them.

Perhaps their hard little hearts would have softened a little if they could have known how their rudeness hurt and disappointed Miss Prince, and how lonely she felt without her own friendly Cubs. But she didn't let them see; she was always cheerful and patient.

A week passed like this, and Miss Prince, who had been determined not to give in, began to despair. Being kind to them was no use; punishing them was no use. Their grandfather was furious, and told Miss Prince that he saw she could not manage them. A friend of his had told him Miss Prince could manage forty fierce Wolf Cubs, and he had said she would easily be able to tame three little boys, however wild. But she had failed; it was not much use to go on trying. Then Miss Prince got a brilliant idea.

"Mr. Ogden," she said, "I think I know a way in which those boys could be altogether changed and made into really good little chaps."

Mr. Ogden grunted like a cross bear. "Do you?" he said. "I don't."

"Will you give a trial to my plan?" said Miss Prince.

"I'll try anything under the sun," said Mr. Ogden. "What's your plan?"

"It is to let me write and engage a boy I know, named Danny Moore, to come and act as companion to the boys, and their own groom. Jones, tells me he needs help with their ponies, and is too old to go out riding with them much longer. This boy is a Patrol-leader in the Scouts. I have known him ever since he was quite a little chap. He is a splendid leader, and can manage the most difficult boys and turn them into good Scouts. He has a good knowledge of horses too. I know he would come at once if I wrote to him, and if it's possible to do anything with your grandsons, Danny will do it."

"Do as you like," said Mr. Ogden sourly. "I wash my hands of the whole business."

That night Miss Prince posted a letter to Danny. In it she told him of the almost hopeless job she had got—of taming three perfect little terrors. She asked him to come and turn them into Wolf Cubs for her. She told him to bring his uniform, and that she would tell him the plan she had made for the way he was first to see them when he arrived.

Danny answered that he would be there in three days, and Miss Prince's hopes began to rise.

CHAPTER IV

"DANNY THE DETECTIVE"

Two days later, the boys having been even worse than usual, Miss Prince shut the door firmly and said: "Now, boys, I am going to give you a new punishment for this disgraceful behaviour. I am going to sit on the floor, and you three are to sit on the floor in a row in front of me, for twenty minutes, and keep perfectly silent."

"Not much!" said Bill, with his cheekiest air.

Miss Prince sat down on the floor. "There was once a boy called Danny," she began. "He was always known as Danny the Detective by his friends. One day a wonderful adventure happened to him." The three boys stopped whistling and listened. Miss Prince went on, talking very quietly. They had to come nearer to hear. It got so thrilling, and they got so excited about Danny and the German spies, that before long they were sitting on the floor, as silent as mice, their eyes fixed on Miss Prince. More than half-an-hour had passed before the story was finished. Then they realized that for once they had done as they had been told, and they began to be as rude as ever.

"Of course, all that is a pack of lies!" said Bill.

David's eyes were shining with excitement; he did so wish he was Danny himself. But he felt he ought to support his twin and keep up the frightfulness, so he made a rude remark, too.

"Danny is now a Scout," said Miss Prince. "He is very fond of camping out in the wood and cooking his meals in a billy-can on a wood fire. Perhaps you will come across him one day when you are in Prior's Wood. But I'm afraid he would not want you as his friends—you're so awfully rude and selfish. I'm afraid he'd call you 'little Huns'!"

"I don't believe anything about Danny," said Bill.

"Nor do I," said the other two. But in their hearts they decided to visit Prior's Wood.

It was the day after this strange new punishment had taken place. Bill, David and Nipper were having tea in the Playroom, when Miss Prince, who had looked anxiously out of the window many times during the last half-hour, heard the wheels of the dog-cart on the drive, and hurried downstairs. The cart had driven round to the stables, and there Miss Prince followed it.

As she came up, a boy had just jumped out, and was taking a kit bag from under the seat. He was a boy of fifteen, medium height, with a very sunburnt, cheery face, and eyes that looked straight at you when he talked, as if he had never had anything to hide or be ashamed of.

"Hullo, Miss Prince!" he cried, with a grin.

"Hullo, Danny!" she said. "How nice to see you again! You seem just like a bit of home!"

She led him into the house, through the great, oak-panelled hall, to her own little sitting-room. There they had a long talk. When they came out Danny was laughing.

"I think it's a splendid plan," he said. "I'll do my best to make it come off successfully."

CHAPTER V

IN THE WOODS

It was a glorious autumn morning—one of those mornings when the wind seems to have swept the world very clean, the sky is very blue and clear of clouds, the sun shines on the red-and-gold leaves, and you feel happy just to be alive. The boys woke up feeling almost good, but, remembering the campaign of frightfulness against Miss Prince which they were determined to carry out, they asked each other what they should do to-day.

"I'll tell you what," said David. "She said she was going to start a new plan for lessons this morning. It would annoy her awfully if we ran away all the morning, and she couldn't start her precious plan! It's such a ripping day, why should we sit in a stuffy schoolroom?"

"Right you are!" said Bill. "I vote we go and play wild buffaloes with Farmer Tomkinson's calves. He's just bought a lot of new ones, and if we let them out on to the heath, we could have some jolly good sport—especially if we take the dogs and the long carriage whip."

"I shan't come with you," said Nipper. "I have a plan of my own."

"Out with it, kid!" said Bill, twisting his small brother's arm till he started his siren-shriek.

"Let go!" he yelled, "and I'll tell you. I'm going to explore Prior's Wood. Don't you remember that story she told us? And she said we might find the Scout if we went in Prior's Wood."

"I think," said Bill, "we'll leave the calves for to-day, and go to Prior's Wood. It's probably all a pack of lies, but we might as well go and see."

And so, after breakfast, before Miss Prince had time to call them for lessons the three boys ran out across the fields to the wood. They had not gone far when David stopped short.

"Hush!" he said. "Squat down before he sees us—quick!"

The other two followed his example, and squatted down, peering cautiously over a clump of bracken.

They had reached a little clearance in the wood, where the ground was carpeted with soft green moss, and a small stream gurgled noisily along. On the banks of the stream was a little hut, built of branches and bracken, between the trunks of three trees.

A little distance from this a bright wood fire burned, sending a steady column of blue smoke up into the sunny air. A billy-can boiled away, standing on a thick piece of wood, whilst on a big, moss-covered log sat a boy. He had bare, brown knees and bare, brown arms and a khaki shirt, his red neckerchief making a bright splash of colour among the greens and browns of the wood. He had a knife in his hand, and he was carving wonderful patterns on a straight ash stick he had cut for himself. As he worked he whistled softly.

The three boys, squatting in the ferns, watched him. Presently he got up and added some wood to his fire, and peeped into the boiling pot. Then he fetched an apple out of his hut, and sat down again on the log. Suddenly a robin swooped down on to a twig quite close, and stared with big, bright eyes at this boy who had come to share his own particular corner of Prior's Wood.

The boy, just as if he knew the language of robins, began to whistle, very softly, in little trills. The robin cocked his head on one side and answered with much the same kind of whistle. Then he swooped down on to the end of the very log Danny was sitting on, and they went on with their whistling conversation.

"I believe he can talk to the birds!" whispered Nipper, with round eyes.

Just then an enormous water rat appeared on the opposite bank of the stream, and began swimming across. Bill's hand shot out instinctively for a stone.

"Shut up, you ass!" said David.

"But I could just hit him on the head beautifully," said Bill.

"Sh—sh! The Scout will kill him, I expect, when he gets nearer. Let's see how he does it," whispered David.

But, strange to say, the Scout, after watching the big rat land, moved noiselessly across to his hut, and came out with a bit of cheese, a little piece of which he poked softly across to the bank with the end of his stick. The rat had vanished. But before long he came out, fetched the piece of cheese, and ran back to his hole. The Scout put another crumb, nearer this time. The rat came out and fetched that. Gradually he came nearer and nearer.

Presently he got so bold that he stayed and ate the crumbs of cheese quite close to Danny—and then sat up and cleaned his whiskers with his little pink hands, and seemed to be combing his fur and brushing his little round ears.

The three boys watched, fascinated. They had never before thought of making friends with a water rat and watching his habits. Their first thought had always been to kill the happy little creature, who was out enjoying the morning sunshine.

Suddenly Nipper could sit still no longer; he stretched his legs, which broke a rotten twig and made such a noise that Danny looked round and saw the three heads watching him through the bracken.

"Hullo!" he said. "Come and see my little camp." He smiled and looked so friendly that the three boys got up and came half-shyly out into the open space.

CHAPTER VI

THE LAW OF THE WOLF CUB PACK

The mysterious boy of the woods took them into his hut, and showed them how it was built. Then he let them put wood on his fire, and after that he gave them each an apple.

"You pinched those from old Crookedshank's, I know!" said Bill.

Danny looked surprised. "No," he said; "I bought them from Mr. Cruikshank."

"You silly!" said David. "He's as deaf as a post, and there's a big hole in his fence just by the apple-tree. Fancy buying apples!"

"Then you would have stolen them from a very poor and deaf old man? What a dirty trick! Besides, stealing is a sin, and no chap with a sense of honour would do it." He looked very serious, and for the first time in their lives the boys felt really ashamed of themselves and had nothing to say.

But Danny had changed the subject. He showed them how to carve sticks. He told them all sorts of things about birds and squirrels and rats. But first of all he made them each a bow and some arrows, with pheasants' and pigeons' feathers, which they found in the woods, to make them go straight.

"I wish we could always stay with you," said Nipper suddenly, "and live out in the woods, and learn to talk to the birds, and shoot with our bows, and be always happy, with no more rows and jawings and punishments."

"Yes!" said David and Bill together. "And could you make us Scouts? We'd win lots of badges."

Danny laughed. "You're too young to be Scouts," he said, "but you might be Wolf Cubs. Who are you?"

"We live up at the Hall," said David. "Mr. Ogden is our grandfather."

"Oho!" said Danny. "So you're the little terrors I've heard so much about!"

The boys hung their heads.

"My word! you're not the sort of chaps they have in the Cubs!" he continued. "From all I hear, you seem to be regular little Bolsheviks! Do you know, Cubs have to do a good turn for somebody every day, but you seem to do a bad turn to somebody every day—and more than one, too."

The boys were silent.

"Squat down," said Danny, "and I'll tell you a bit about Cubs. It's not all play, you know. Chaps who join the Cubs have to behave decently, whether they're in uniform or not. Once you've taken the Cub Promise, you're a Cub all the time, day and night. The Cubs have two laws they've got to keep. One is obedience—they promise to obey the grown-ups. Could you do that?"

"We never have," said Bill, digging his fingers into the moss, "but we could if we tried."

"Then the second law says you mustn't give in to yourself— that means, you mustn't do all you feel like doing, whether it's right or wrong. You mustn't steal Mr. Cruikshank's apples, and say rude things to people, and tell lies, and fight each other."

"It would be very hard to keep all that," said Nipper, "but it would be worth it—to be Cubs."

"And I think perhaps we should be happier," said David thoughtfully. "I'm tired of doing frightfulness against Miss

Prince."

Then Danny told them about the Promise—first, loyalty to God. But they had to admit they never thought about God at all, never said morning or night prayers, never went to church, never did anything in order to please God.

Danny looked very serious. "Poor little chaps!" he said suddenly. "But you'll learn to do better now, and God will forgive you for being so selfish and ungrateful."

He told them a lot more about Cubs, and their eyes shone with excitement.

"If we come down here after dinner, will you make us into Cubs?" said David.

Danny laughed. "A Cub isn't made as quickly as all that," he said. "You will have to show you're worthy of taking the Cub Promise and can keep the Cub Law. Oughtn't you to be at lessons this afternoon?"

"Yes," said the boys.

"Well," said Danny, "if you go back and tell Miss Prince you're very sorry you ran away this morning and beg her pardon, and then do your best at lessons this afternoon, you can ask her if you may come down here and have tea with me. Will you do that?"

It seemed to them very hard, but they said they would. And so the three boys went back to dinner with very new thoughts in their minds.

"I think," said David, as they neared the house, "that we've been beasts all our lives, and somehow I didn't see it till that Scout was talking."

And so they went and found Miss Prince, and had it all out with her; and she forgave them freely, and they all shook hands and vowed friendship and loyalty for the future. At lessons they tried their very hardest and did quite well. Then they rushed down and had a glorious tea in the woods by

Danny's camp-fire.

"I'll come home with you," said Danny, when the evening began to close in.

"Hooray!" shouted the boys.

"Because you see," said Danny, "I'm living at the Hall, too. Mr. Ogden has engaged me to be your companion and groom." The boys went nearly mad with delight.

And as they walked home together, while the sun set in a glory of red and gold, and purple shadows crept out of the woods, they talked of how the boys would become Cubs—real, true, and faithful Cubs; and how they would get a few more and make a little Pack, and ask Miss Prince to be the Cubmaster.

That evening, when it had got dark and they were all squatting round the fire on the floor, Nipper suddenly said, "Are you Danny the Detective?"

"Yes," laughed Danny. Then the Cubs fell on him, and smacked him on the back, and nearly tore him to pieces.

"Tell us your adventures," said David. And so Danny began to tell them of his Cub days and the German spies.

And Miss Prince, looking at the happy group, said, in her heart, "Thank God!"

CHAPTER VII

A WOLF CUB COUNCIL

A Council was in progress; and once again it was in the old pigsty. But this time it was not a Council of War; frightfulness and rebellion were not the questions under discussion. No, it was a Wolf Cub Council, and Danny was seated upon the Council Rock—a huge boulder the boys had managed to drag into the pigsty with the help of one of the under-gardeners.

"I have a proposal to bring forward," said Danny. "The Council (you're the Council) can vote upon it when I have explained it. If you want to be Cubs we must form a Six. That means getting three more boys. I have kept my eyes open the last few days, and I have three names to propose."

This was a splendid Council—it was so serious and important. The boys wriggled with excitement.

"Who do you propose?" said David.

"I propose, first, Hugh Burnett, the gamekeeper's son. He's a jolly good chap, and knows the woods and the surrounding country very thoroughly. All the people round think a lot of him. I should say he's a born Cub."

"Yes," said Bill. "I think Hugh is all right. His father used to be our chief enemy, and chase us out of the woods. Once he gave David a thrashing for taking a nest of pheasants' eggs. But he seems nicer now."

"Then I suggest Jack Miles, the blacksmith's boy. He's a regular sport. I don't believe he's afraid of anything in the world. He ought to make a good Cub with a bit of training."

"Yes," said David. "He and Bill had the worst fight I ever saw, once. He made Bill's nose bleed; it went on for half-an-hour. Bill broke one of his front teeth. He gave Bill a jolly good whacking, too!"

"Good!" said Danny, "that'll probably mean they will be better friends now."

Nipper was beginning to look anxious. "They're all so big," he said. "It's bad enough having Bill and David, but with all that lot, what'll happen to me?"

"I've thought of you, kid," said Danny. "There's a nice little chap would make a pair for you—Bobby Brown, Dr. Brown's son. He's only just eight, and a bit quiet, but you chaps will soon put some life into him."

"Hooray, hooray!" said Nipper; "he'll be my ally, and we won't half show you fellows something."

"Don't forget the Cub spirit," said Danny; "there's going to be no more bullying now. Besides, the younger ones mustn't show cheek to the Sixer and Second. Who will second my motion?"

David seconded the proposals, and the rest of the Council was unanimous.

"Carried," said Danny. "Now let's go and ask the boys if they'll join the Six."

CHAPTER VIII

"I PROMISE...."

The great day had come at last—the day when the six Cubs were to make their Promise. The gamekeeper, the blacksmith, and the doctor had said "Yes, certainly," about their sons joining, and of course Hugh, Jack, and Bob were wild with delight at the idea. Mr. Ogden had grunted, and said, "Anything to keep them out of mischief," when Miss Prince asked his leave to form the Six, and when she had mentioned something about funds, he had given her a £5 note. The order for kit was posted to headquarters, and to-day the boys were clad in dark blue jerseys, shorts (real short ones), and green neckerchiefs, and smart Cub caps.

When the question of a Sixer and Second came up Bill and David had announced, both at the same time, that he would be Sixer; but Danny had told them not to be so jolly cocksure, for he and Miss Prince had talked the matter over very seriously and decided to give Hugh the two stripes; for, as Danny said, he was a good chap, and would, he was sure, make a proper Sixer, always thinking of his Six before himself and trying to set a good example to the other boys.

David was to be Hugh's Second; Bill (his twin), being the next oldest, took third place; Jack Miles, fourth; Nipper, fifth; and little Bobby Brown sixth.

And so they stood in a circle on this sunny Saturday afternoon, and Miss Prince, in Cubmaster's uniform, stood before them with Danny at her side, six badges in his hand.

Hugh was the first to come up. Standing at the half-salute, a look of determination on his face, he repeated the Promise slowly, clearly, and as if he said it with all his heart. As Miss Prince looked into his truthful blue eyes, she felt sure that he really meant the words he had said and would keep true to them all his life.

"I trust you to keep that Promise," she said, adding, as she clasped his left hand, "you are now a Cub and a member of the great Brotherhood of Scouts." Danny put his cap on for him, and Miss Prince gave him the badge.

Then he brought up each of his boys in turn. They all said the Promise clearly, and with a true intention of keeping it. Then they gave the Grand Howl.

"Now, Cubs," said Miss Prince, "you mustn't forget that you've got to uphold the honour of the Brotherhood. To-morrow morning," she added, "we will all go to church together in uniform, and you must renew your Promise before God, and ask Him to help you to keep it faithfully as long as you live."

Then the Circle was dismissed, and the newly-made Cubs dashed off across the lawn, turning head over heels as they went. There was a splendid tea laid out on the terrace, with a huge plum cake that was the birthday cake of the Pack.

The following Saturday was a holiday. They had chosen, of course, to spend it in the woods with Danny. In the afternoon the three other Cubs joined them, and a fire-lighting competition began. Danny was to be the judge of the fires—he was to give points in getting a good fire burning for speed, and for the way the fireplace had been made. So while the Cubs worked hard, he sat on a log and thought.

He liked his new job. It was great fun training this keen little lot of Cubs; and he was so pleased to be able to help Miss Prince in this way. But as he thought over things there was something that puzzled him. The boys' grandfather was such a strange old man. No one ever saw him smile, or got a pleasant word from him. The village people hated him; he was a hard landlord and a harder master. And somehow he never seemed happy, though he was rich, and had a beautiful house and all a man could desire.

"He looks to me," said Danny to himself, "as if he was always afraid, always dreading something—as if he had an awful secret weighing on his conscience." And then the detective instinct in him began weaving mysterious stories around the gloomy figure of Mr. Ogden. Little did he think, however, that before many months had passed a strange adventure would befall him which should clear away the mystery surrounding the Cubs' grandfather. It was a call from Nipper that brought him back to the present—"Danny, Danny, I've done!" Before long the six fires were complete and the judging had commenced.

It was actually Nipper's fire that won! He had had the luck to find some large smooth stones with which to build his fireplace. Also he had had the happy thought of borrowing Danny's hat to fan his fire with. Now he strutted with pride like a young turkey-cock.

"All bring your wood," said Danny, "and pile it on to Nipper's fire. We will boil the water on it for tea."

Before long tea was made and the seven boys were squatting round ready to begin. It was then that a figure came on the scene—a figure whose coming was the beginning of a long series of adventures such as the Cubs had never even dreamed of.

CHAPTER IX

THE COMING OF THE MYSTERIOUS TRAMP

He came down the little path, through the bracken, walking rather unsteadily, like a man who is weak from illness or hunger. The evening sun, slanting through the trees, fell on his shabby figure. He halted as he saw the Cubs, and stood irresolute, as though wondering whether he should go back or proceed. The Cubs, turning from their fire, gazed in surprise at the intruder. But at first they did not notice his ragged appearance, for something in his face, his eyes, held them. His face was very thin, but it was a beautiful face. He had very clear, grey eyes—mysterious eyes that seemed to be looking away into the invisible—looking for something they never found. There was something very sad about his face, but there was also something about it that made the boys feel that he was a friend.

All this was the first impression that the man gave them as their eyes met. The next moment they were looking him over critically. With this look they noticed that his clothes were torn and ragged, his boots nearly worn out, but that he was very clean and carefully shaved, and had very white hands with long fingers. "Hands like an artist," said Danny to himself. The man turned about as if to go back along the path, but Danny jumped up and stepped towards him. This mysterious stranger could not be allowed to go away like this. There was something about him that appealed strongly to Danny's imagination.

"I say, sir," he said (the sir came out involuntarily), "won't you come and have some tea by our fire?"

The man turned, surprised, and then meeting Danny's eager eyes, smiled.

"Well," he said, "it's very good of you to ask me—I'm afraid I'm trespassing."

"No, you aren't," said Danny, "come on. Fill up that mug, David, and pass the grub along. Won't you sit on this log, sir?"

The man sat down close to the fire. He took the mug Danny handed to him and a large slice of bread and butter. This he ate in silence—he was evidently very hungry. The boys watched him. No one spoke. At last Nipper broke the silence.

"Who are you?" he said.

"A tramp," replied the man.

Once again silence fell. Then Nipper broke it again.

"You aren't a very ordinary kind of tramp," he said. "I think we will call you the mysterious tramp. You will stay with us, won't you, and tell us things? We were just wanting an adventure."

The man smiled. His smile came slowly, as if it was rusty from long disuse. And David decided that he was so queer and silent because he had probably lived for many years upon a desert island and forgotten how to talk.

"Am I an adventure?" said the man. "And what things do you want me to tell you? Stories, I suppose. I used to tell stories once, but I've forgotten them all. There was a little kid I—I knew. She was always pestering me for stories. But that was long ago."

"Oh, do try and remember them," said the Cubs, crowding round him. The tea and bread and butter and birthday cake seemed to have cheered up the mysterious tramp no end, and he seemed to be remembering how to talk. Before long he was even laughing.

By dint of much questioning the Cubs managed to discover quite a lot about him. That he had once been an artist, for one thing, and could still draw fascinating little pictures with bits of burnt wood on smooth, flat stones. He seemed to like drawing little girls better than boys, which was a pity. They also discovered that once he had lived in a little house on the edge of a wood, and could make the calls of cuckoos and wood-pigeons by blowing through his clasped hands. Also he knew all sorts of things about the habits of fox cubs and squirrels and hedgehogs.

The sun sank down behind the distant woods. The autumn evening closed in, blue and misty. The harvest moon crept up, orange-coloured and enormous above the trees. But still the Cubs and the mysterious tramp sat in the red glow of the fire. Nipper was on the tramp's knees, and Hugh and David sat pressed up against his legs. Bill, the practical one, kept stoking the fire so as to prevent the party coming to an end.

Suddenly David gripped the tramp's leg. "Look—a ghost!" he whispered; but Danny laughed. "It's Miss Prince coming to look for you," he said.

Miss Prince, a white scarf thrown over her dark hair, stepped out of the shadow of the trees into the circle of light.

"You are having a late birthday party, kiddies," she said. Then she saw the stranger by the light of the fire, and stared at him in surprised silence.

"This," said Nipper, putting his arms round the man's neck, "is our mysterious tramp, and that," he said, with a nod of his head, "is Miss Prince. She's very nice, really."

The mysterious tramp got up and stepped back into the blue darkness beyond the bright glow of the fire.

"It's time you kids were in bed," he said, "and that I was back on the roads."

"Yes," said Miss Prince, "come along."

The Cubs were about to raise a cry of protest, when Danny whispered "Cub Law." This was the secret sign between them when they forgot.

"All right, Miss Prince," said Bill. "But let us just say good night to our tramp." They pressed round him. "You will come back to-morrow, won't you?" they pleaded.

"No, no," said the man. "I must go back to the roads. But it's been awfully jolly, to-night. Thank you for being pals. I shan't forget you, kiddies."

Very reluctantly the Cubs went away with Miss Prince, but Danny did not go with them. Stepping out of the circle of light into the shadow, he walked down the path, where in the yellow moonlight he could see a dark figure ahead. The mysterious tramp was not going to escape so easily.

CHAPTER X

BY MOONLIGHT

For a moment Danny stood on the path, just beyond the red glow of the fire, and wondered what he should do. He could hear the voices of the Cubs telling Miss Prince all about the mysterious tramp and the crackling of their steps as they walked away through the bracken fern and undergrowth. Ahead, along the path, he could see a dark figure walking a little unsteadily.

The moon had mounted higher in the grey, star-pricked sky. Mystery, adventure, romance—Danny felt it was very near, and yet it was walking away from him, a black figure, silhouetted against a silvery distance. He must stop it from going—but how?

Without knowing exactly what he meant to do he began running, and had soon caught up the tramp.

"Sir," he said, "I say, sir!"

The man turned round. "Well?" he said in his strange, sad voice.

"I wish you wouldn't go away," said Danny.

"Why?" said the tramp.

"Well, because—because we've just made friends, and if you go tramping along the roads we may never see you again. Besides, it's going to be a cold night, and you won't have anywhere to sleep. And I don't believe you ought to be tramping with nothing to eat. You look as if you were ill."

The man had turned, and was looking at Danny curiously.

"You're right," he said. "The roads are all very well when you've got money or food, and the nights are warm. But I've only had one meal in the last two days. I hate begging. When they give—and give with a smile—it's all right. But when they refuse—well, I can't ask again that day." He shivered, and drew his tattered coat closer round him.

"Come back to the fire," said Danny, "then we can talk. I'll show you a good place to spend the night. When you've had a bit of a rest and some grub you'll feel better."

Half reluctantly the tramp followed him back to the fire, and sat down once more on the log.

There was silence for a few minutes. Then the tramp spoke.

"I don't know why you are so kind to me," he said. "Do you know, while I sat there, with a kiddy on my knee, and the others round, I was happy again—I seemed to forget everything, as one forgets a bad dream."

Danny poked the fire with his foot. "What was your bad dream?" he asked.

The tramp did not answer for a very long time. Then he said: "I've never told it to any one. In fact it's over seven years since I spoke to any one as a friend. I will tell it to you, as you have asked me to. Silence is best—but just for once, sympathy is good. My bad dream is a spoiled life, and seven years in prison."

Danny gasped. Then, as the tramp was silent, he stirred the fire up into a blaze and drew nearer to him.

"It wasn't your fault, was it, sir?" he said. "Tell me the story."

CHAPTER XI

THE TRAMP'S STORY

"I lived," said the tramp, "in a little house on the edge of a wood just outside a village. I had a little daughter. She was more like a fairy than a child. Her mother died when she was a wee girl. I was an artist. I used to paint pictures of the woods and lanes and trees—the woods by moonlight, the woods at sunrise, the woods all green and blue in spring; the woods looking like dark, solemn churches on winter afternoons, with the red and gold and purple sunset showing through the fine black traceries of the trees like the stained-glass windows of a Gothic cathedral, and blue mist hanging about like incense. And somehow there were always fairies peeping out somewhere in my pictures—Mariette expected them. And after all, what are artists for if not to see what ordinary people miss and put what they see into their pictures? We had no friends, Mariette and I—we didn't want any. We had each other and the fairies.

"Sometimes I used to spend the night out in the woods, getting pictures into my head to paint by day, or so as to catch the very first glimmer of golden clouds for a picture of the sunrise fairies. I used to leave Mariette at the cottage of my old nurse, whom she loved very much. It was on one of these sunrise days that my bad dreams began.

"Mariette was just seven. I had left her with the old nurse, and had started out to spend a night in the woods about five miles away. I took a few things with me so as to camp in the bracken, and be fresh and ready to paint at dawn. As I walked through the village, I chanced to meet a man that Mariette and I always called 'the wicked uncle.' He was the only person in the place that we did not like. He lived in a square, grey house, with dirty windows, and most of the blinds drawn down. He had a mean, cruel face, and little eyes like a rat. We were quite sure no fairies lived in his garden—it was a sad, dull garden, with no flowers.

"As I passed him that evening at dusk, he said, 'Good evening. Going on a painting expedition?' 'Yes,' I said. 'But surely,' said the wicked uncle, 'you can't paint by moonlight?' 'No,' I replied, 'I am going to sleep out in the woods, and paint at sunrise.' 'Oh,' he said, 'and what happens to your little girl?' 'She stays with Mrs. Binks,' I answered. I was getting tired of his questions. 'Going far?' he called after me. I had grown impatient. 'Yes, miles and miles,' I shouted. I felt angry to think of his having pried into our private affairs. Somehow I did not sleep well on my bracken bed. I kept seeing the face of 'the wicked uncle,' and his little peering eyes in the dusk.

"After sunrise I painted for a few hours, and then started home. It was nine when I reached Mrs. Binks' cottage, where I had gone to call for Mariette to come back and help me cook my breakfast. But she was not there, nor was Mrs. Binks.

"I went on to our cottage, but they were not there either. So I made myself some tea and fried an egg, and just as I was sitting down to begin, I heard the sound of feet on the cobbled path outside. It was a strange, tramping sound, and I expected to hear a rap on my knocker. But to my surprise the door was opened from outside, and for a moment I saw the cunning face of the 'wicked uncle.'

"Then a police inspector and three constables marched in. I was too much surprised to speak. It was the inspector who broke the silence. 'I arrest you,' he said, 'on a charge of forgery.' Click, click, and handcuffs were on my wrists.

"Of course, I said I knew nothing about forgery, and was pretty rude, too, I'm afraid, as I was angry. But the inspector laughed drily, and said he had a very clear case against me. I was not quite such a clever fellow as I thought. In a moment there would be some very pretty evidence, so I had better leave off arguing. 'Lead the way, Mr. Crale,' he added, turning to the 'wicked uncle,' who thereupon produced a bunch of skeleton keys and led the way through my kitchen, followed by the inspector and two constables.

"I told the two bobbies who were left to guard me exactly what I thought of Mr. Crale; but they grinned at my remarks, and one of them said: ''E's done a good turn to us police, anyway. A long time we've been searching for the ringleader of your gang, and we shouldn't never have found you if it 'adn't 'a' been for Mr. Crale. A clever gentleman he is.'

"Just then the party came back. I had heard them stumping down my cellar stairs. They carried three great chests which Mr. Crale unlocked with his skeleton keys. One contained an enormous number of bank notes. Another a curious set of instruments I could not understand. A third was full of letters and papers. 'A very pretty little press you've got down there,' said the inspector. 'We'll come back for that, later.'

"Well, to make a long story short, I was taken away in a motor car. I begged to be allowed to see Mariette, but Mr. Crale told the inspector I had sent Mariette away the day before to stay with some friend in London, and was only trying to find a way to escape by asking to see her now. I was tried, and the case against me was extraordinarily clever. There were papers and letters and documents all pointing to my guilt; and when I pleaded not guilty, and accused Crale of being the forger himself, and of using me to cover his own guilt, they only smiled, as much as to say what a fool I was to go on denying what was so obvious.

"When I said I must see Mariette and Mrs. Binks they

told me it was no use talking like that, as they had my letter in their possession making over my daughter to one of my accomplices, who had unfortunately managed to escape, and had my daughter with him. And so I was cast into prison, and all that I had—not much—was taken to pay my supposed debts.

"There were no fairies in prison, nor Mariette. But the worst—the worst thing of all was that I did not know what had become of her. I nearly went mad. Before long I became very ill. Nearly a year I spent in the prison infirmary. Then I served six long years in the cells. Three months ago I was set free."

The tramp's clear, sad voice ceased. Danny was breathing hard. Bitter rage filled his soul. He dared not speak, for he felt the words he would utter would not be Scout-like. Then he remembered that the man had said he wanted sympathy. He did not know what to say—no words could possibly express the sympathy he felt. He gripped the tramp's cold hand. "No one can know how ghastly it must be for you, sir," he said huskily; "no one, except God."

Silence fell between them. The fire had burned very low. At last Danny spoke. "Why are you a tramp?" he said.

"Because," said the man slowly, "I have a quest—two quests. The first is to find my little Mariette. Day and night in prison I dreamed of finding her. When I came out I just started walking and walking, looking for her. I have no money to travel in any other way. I know no trade. All I could do was to paint, and I can't paint now. You must have a happy heart to paint pictures of woods and fairies. And so I tramp and tramp, and pray every day that God will guide me to where my little Mariette is waiting for her daddy to find her in this long game of hide-and-seek.

"Do you know, whenever I come to a cross-road I kneel down and pray with all my heart to God to make me take the right road that will lead me to her at last. Then I turn round three times with my eyes shut and take the road I face. When I came down that little path towards your fire it was because when I opened my eyes I was not facing any road but the stile into the wood. I took the path, somehow feeling that something was going to happen.”

“Perhaps God sent you this way because He means us to find Mariette for you. Did you notice the little grey church near the cross-roads?”

“Yes, yes,” said the tramp, “that was why I felt I must take the path. I saw the statue of St. Antony over the door—St. Antony, the saint who finds lost things.”

“Yes,” said Danny, “I thought of that, too.”

The tramp stood up. Then suddenly he laughed an almost happy laugh. “‘Danny the Detective,’ the Cubs called you,” he said. “Well, Danny, it’s done me good to talk to you. And I believe between you and St. Antony I shall get my little fairy back again. God is very good.”

So Danny led the mysterious tramp through the wood to a deserted cottage that a gamekeeper had once lived in. He gathered some dry bracken and with this and his own camp blankets made him a bed. A good supper of steak pie and potatoes and roly-poly pudding had been kept hot for Danny by the kind old cook. That night the tramp enjoyed the best meal he had had for seven years; but he did not know that Danny went to bed on a supper of biscuits left over from tea.

A bottle made a fine candlestick, and the old cottage looked quite cosy by the time Danny had finished arranging it.

“Good night, sir,” he said at last. “I hope you’ll sleep well. To-morrow we must have a proper pow-wow about things. My word, the Cubs won’t half be pleased to find you here.”

CHAPTER XII

THE SECOND QUEST

The dew lay thick and white on the grass; hips and haws made bright splashes of colour in the early morning sunlight; the robins sang, the larks soared, the woodpeckers tapped— but Danny noticed none of them. With his hands behind him and his head bent, he walked across the field, deep in thought.

Last night, with the pale moon and the red glow of the fire, and the tramp's sad story, all seemed like a strange dream. And what he had said, himself, seemed like a dream too, for he had promised the tramp that he would undertake to find his lost daughter.

Somehow he felt so sure that he was meant to do so. He had asked the tramp to stay in the deserted cottage for the night, and promised to have a pow-wow the next day as to how they should commence the search.

But in the morning light things did not seem so possible and easy. After all, it was seven years ago that the girl had vanished. She had been stolen, too, by malicious people; and the scene of the plot against the artist was many miles away.

The police and the court had been fooled by the gang of forgers, and had refused to make any inquiries about the artist's little girl. It would be a hopeless quest for a Scout to start asking questions about an ex-convict's past. What on earth could Danny say to the tramp?

He had reached Prior's Wood, and still no idea had occurred to him. All he could think of was that they should get their poor friend to stay there awhile, and recover his strength and his spirits. It might be possible, then, to get him work or perhaps he would feel able to begin painting again, and get a job in that line.

When Danny reached the cottage the tramp was sitting outside it in the sun. His hair was all wet from his wash in the stream. He looked, somehow, quite happy, and he seemed so absorbed in his own day-dreams that he did not notice Danny as he came up, until he said "Good morning!"

"Hullo, Danny!" he replied. "I've slept better on your bracken bed than I've done for many years. And I've dreamed—oh, such lovely dreams! All about my little Mariette. I feel quite happy again. It's made me long to paint again, and I've been finding no end of pictures in this wood, ever since sunrise!"

Danny laughed, but he felt more like crying inside. There was so little chance of finding the girl, and yet the tramp was beginning to count on it as if it was already done.

But somehow Danny felt that he was meant to find the girl, and his spirits rose. For nearly an hour he and the artist-tramp discussed pictures. Then Danny made a fire, and boiled a billy of tea, and produced a loaf and some butter out of his haversack.

"About twelve o'clock," he said, "you'll have six wild Wolf Cubs descending upon you. They yelled with joy when I told them their 'mysterious tramp' was still here! Now I must get back and take them to church."

So he said good-bye to the tramp and went back to the house, whistling.

Out of the little grey church at the cross-roads came the Cubs, very demurely. But no sooner were they outside the churchyard gate than they gave vent to a wild yell, and, tumbling over the stile, tore off down the path to the gamekeeper's cottage.

When Danny arrived with the big basket of lunch, he found them very happy. The tramp had apparently turned into a most dangerous grizzly bear, and the Cubs into intrepid hunters.

All the afternoon their mysterious friend told them stories. When at last it was time for them to go Danny saw them home, and then came back to the cottage. He stoked up the fire and sat down by it.

"Sir," he said, "when you told me your story last night, you said you were tramping the roads because you have two quests. One was to find your little girl. You did not tell me the other."

The tramp's face clouded. His kind grey eyes suddenly became as hard as steel. He did not answer for some time. Then he spoke slowly.

"My second quest is this," he said; "to find the fellow who wronged me, and reap my revenge!"

Danny was taken aback. This was so different from the kind, jolly artist of this morning. Suddenly he realized a little the bitterness of soul produced by those seven years' unjust confinement, and by the cruel loss of his child.

He saw the whole story in a new light and understood it better. More than ever did he long to help this man, and yet those words, spoken so deliberately, filled him with horror. Revenge is a grievous sin. How could this man pray every day to find his daughter, and expect God to hear his prayers, while, in his heart of hearts, there was revenge?

"Well," said the tramp, staring at Danny, "what's the matter?"

"Oh, sir," cried Danny, "then we shall never find Mariette!"

"What do you mean?" said the tramp.

"I mean," said Danny, "that the only possible chance of finding her is for God to answer your prayers. And He won't do that till you forgive your enemies."

The tramp scowled darkly.

"You're only a boy," he said; "you don't understand. There are some things a man can't forgive."

There was nothing more to be said. Danny's heart was heavy as he went to bed that night.

The next morning Danny was very busy. He had been given the job of clipping the three ponies, and he was not able to go down to the wood. He was just about to set out, at one o'clock, when Miss Prince called him into her sitting-room.

"I want to speak to you, Danny," she said. "I was down in the village just now, taking the boys to their carpentry class, and as I came back, alone, I met a man at the cross-roads. He came up to me and said, 'Would you, please, give a message to Danny for me? Tell him that the Squire came through the wood, and, finding me in the old gamekeeper's cottage, was furiously angry. He spoke—well, very roughly, and said that if I did not clear out at once he would hand me over to the police. So I'm clearing out.' He looked awfully sad," added Miss Prince, "and just as I was turning away he said, 'Say good-bye to the kiddies for me. They performed a good turn, right enough, when they let me be friends with them.'

"He looked too sad for anything, and so thin and ragged. I gave him a shilling. At first he went very red, and then he took it, and said, 'Thank you very much. I shall keep it as a souvenir of those who were kind to me.' He looked at me as if he wanted to say something else, but he turned away without saying it, and walked down the road. It was the man the Cubs gave tea to on their birthday. What did he mean about the cottage?"

So Danny told Miss Prince how he had made the tramp a bed there. And then, in strict confidence, he told her the whole of the tramp's sad story, because he felt so unhappy about it himself and felt he must talk of it to someone. The tears came into Miss Prince's eyes.

"Cheer up, Danny," she said. "I somehow feel we shall see him again, and that he will forgive his enemies, and that you will find the little girl."

CHAPTER XIII

ELEPHANTS

The golden autumn turned to white winter. Christmas came, with frosty snow, and holly, and Santa Claus, and a party. The holidays ended, and Miss Prince came back.

Then came spring, with little green shoots on the hedges, and catkins, and the first celandines, and all the things that are so thrilling to find again after the long months without them. And the Cubs cut down lots of silver willow-palm to decorate the house on Palm Sunday. Then came May Day. The village children had a maypole. It was a very pretty sight when the little girls danced round it; but there was an awful tragedy when the twins collected all the coloured ribbons into two bunches and played "giant strides" on it, when no one was about! Of course all the ribbons broke, and the twins were not allowed to wear their Cub uniform for a fortnight.

And all this while what had happened to the mysterious tramp? No one knew. He had gone away that autumn morning, and no one had heard of him since.

It was one lovely warm evening in June that Nipper and Bobby Brown suddenly rushed up to where Miss Prince and the twins were weeding the garden, and cried:

"Elephants! Elephants!"

"What on earth do you mean?" said David.

"There's elephants—lots of 'em—coming up the road!" shrieked Nipper.

"Nipper," said Bill sternly, "how can you tell lies like that? Have you forgotten you're a Cub?"

Nipper flushed with indignation.

"There are elephants! There are elephants," he said.

"And camels," added Bobby, "and—and things called unicorns, I think, or is it crocodiles?"

"What do they mean?" said the twins. Just then Danny came on the scene. "I've two bits of news to tell you," he cried. "You'll never guess what! First, the mysterious tramp has come back. He's working for Farmer Higgins, getting in the hay. He is sleeping in one of the barns there."

The Cubs cheered and turned somersaults in their delight.

"The second thing," said Danny, "is that a circus is coming up the road. Caravans, tents, boat-swings, elephants, and all sorts."

"There," cried Nipper, "am I a liar?" But Nipper and Bobby were forgotten in the excitement. Everyone rushed down to the road to see the circus pass, on its way to the village green, where the great tent was to be pitched.

The elephants, led by tiny gipsy boys, with very white teeth and gold rings in their ears, stopped and snuffed at the Cubs with their great, moist trunks. The Cubs gave them bits of bread. And there were camels and dromedaries (not unicorns), and a lion in a cage, and lots and lots of caravans.

"There is going to be a Grand Performance to-morrow afternoon," said Danny. "Buffalo Bill, tight-rope walkers, the lion-taming lady, bare-back riding, and all sorts of good things."

The Cubs' eyes danced with delight. They had never seen a circus in all their lives.

"Oh, Miss Prince!" they cried, and looked at her expectantly.

She laughed. "Yes," she said, "a half-holiday—I know. Well, be very good boys to-morrow morning and earn one.

Then we'll all go to the circus in the afternoon."

They showed their gratitude by pummelling her till she cried for mercy.

Just then a strange figure came by in the procession—a huge man, with a bushy black beard and thick black eyebrows. He was mounted on a great black horse.

"That's Black Bill," said Danny, "the boss of the show. I've often heard of him. Everyone in the circus is awfully afraid of him—even the lion-taming lady!"

The Cubs shrank back as Black Bill passed, for he gave them a stern look. Danny met his eyes, and something seemed to say within him, "You'll see more of Black Bill before you've done."

"Oh, I wish to-morrow would hurry up and come!" said the twins. And all that night they dreamt of the circus.

CHAPTER XIV

THE CIRCUS

"Miss Prince really is a brick!" said Bill, and the others agreed. Miss Prince had earned this highest form of praise by granting a whole holiday on the strength of the circus, the mysterious tramp's return, and the first day's real haymaking.

The circus had passed on up the road to the village green. The horses had been taken out of the shafts and hobbled. Smoke rose in little blue columns from the caravan chimneys. Small brown children, with bare feet, clambered up and down the little ladders that led up to the caravan doors, where their mothers sat—stout ladies, with very black hair and gold rings in their ears.

With much hammering and shouting, an enormous round tent was being pitched in Farmer Brown's field. Also in this field strong men struggled with boat swings, and big boys arranged cocoanut shies. Black Bill strode round calling everybody bad names and making himself generally beastly, but getting the work done in double-quick time.

Of course the entire population of the village looked on. The Cubs, feeling as if some wonderful fairy story had at last come true, stood with wide eyes, drinking it all in. Their blood ran cold as they heard the lion roar. But when they saw the lady who trained him they were not surprised that he obeyed her; she was truly fearsome.

They peered about round the caravan containing the fat lady, in hopes of catching a glimpse of her, but she was apparently too bashful to come out. The first performance was not to take place until the next day, though the "stunts" would be open to the public that evening. The Cubs would have hung round the gipsy camp all day had not Danny made a suggestion.

"Look here," he said, "I vote we go over to Farmer Higgins' now. I hear he is short-handed, and wants to get his hay in while this lovely weather lasts. I believe he would be glad of our help. And then in the dinner hour we will see our tramp, and hear of all he's been doing since he went away."

The thought of haymaking and the tramp was sufficient attraction to draw the cubs away from the circus, and with light hearts they set out for the farm.

Mr. Higgins was delighted to see them. He provided them with pitchforks and big wooden rakes, and said that if they worked very hard that day and got the hay dry enough to cart to-morrow they might have rides on top of the loaded wagons. It had always been a cherished dream of the twins to ride on a hay-cart, but up till now the farmers had been their enemies, and none of them would have allowed "one of 'em terrors" in his field.

"After all," said David reflectively, "it's much jollier being friends with everybody, instead of enemies. I'm glad Miss Prince and Danny came and turned us into Cubs."

They worked like niggers all the morning. Jerseys soon came off, and scarves were turned into a kind of Arab headgear. David and Nipper raked the hay into long lines, and Bill and Danny turned these over with pitchforks.

At about one o'clock the womenfolk belonging to the haymakers began to arrive with dinners tied up in red handkerchiefs.

Suddenly a cheer went up from the Cubs.

"Miss Prince—bringing us dinner!" They were as hungry

as wolves, and it made you feel so like a real farm hand to have your dinner brought you. So they made a camp in a shady corner of the field, and while Miss Prince and the Cubs unpacked the basket, Danny went off in search of the tramp.

Before long they returned together. The tramp still looked very thin, but his face had been burned brown by exposure to the sun during his long hours of farm work. The Cubs leapt at him like a crowd of real young wolves and dragged him down into their hay fort. "Tell us a story!" "No, draw us a picture!" "Make the cuckoo noise; perhaps a real one will answer now!" Everyone shouted at the same time.

The tramp laughed.

"I should say, have some lunch first!" said Miss Prince. "You must all be hungry."

So everybody settled down to ham sandwiches and hard-boiled eggs, and cucumber, and cake, and gooseberry turnovers, and lots and lots of lemonade. Of course the food got all mixed up with hay, grasshoppers, and little wee spiders, but no one seemed to mind.

"A funny thing, my turning up here again, isn't it?" said the tramp. "It was quite by accident. In fact, I didn't know I was coming here until I arrived at the cross-roads, and recognized the place by that little church. A man I worked for, for a few days, said he knew of a farmer friend of his who badly wanted help with his hay, and so he offered to give me a forty-mile lift on a motor-lorry of his that was coming this way. I never asked where the place was, but I felt Providence had meant me to come back when I found myself at those cross-roads again!"

"How did you get on all the winter?" asked Miss Prince.

The tramp shuddered. "Ugh! The winter!" he said. "I want to forget all about that! It's summer now—glorious summer!"

He lay back in a patch of sun.

"I wish it was always summer, and there were always hay

jobs. I've tried my hand at many kinds of work since I saw you last. I'm a huge success as a painter of signs. I couldn't stick begging any longer. By the way," he said, turning to Miss Prince, "that shilling was the last I ever took for doing nothing!"

Miss Prince laughed. She had already noticed that he was wearing a shilling piece on a piece of string round his neck.

"Now it's a mascot?" she said.

"Yes," said the tramp. "I believe if I'd carried it loose I'd have spent it one day. When you're hungry you cease to be superstitious or sentimental."

These long words bored the Cubs.

"Tell us a story!" said the twins, and Nipper suddenly smothered the tramp with an enormous armful of hay.

"No, no," he said, "I must get back to work. Perhaps this evening I will tell you a story—when work's done."

And so haymaking started again, and the Cubs learnt that doing your best can be very hot work, especially when you have a tyrant of a Scout to shout, "Dyb, dyb, dyb!" every time you happen to feel like having a rest or a hayfight.

After tea the Cubs knocked off work and went down to the circus. They swung in the boats till they felt sick, and then rode galloping horses on the roundabout by way of a remedy. They knocked down cocoanuts and won china vases off the hoop-la. They paid 2d. and saw the fat lady—and she was fat! They managed to persuade the man who looked after the animals to let them go round behind, where nobody is allowed to go, and made friends with the white ponies and performing dogs. Then, when it began to get dark and a rough crowd of big boys and farm hands began to come, Danny took them home.

The next day there was to be the great performance—that was what they were longing for.

The next day was as glorious as ever. The hay was to be

carried. The Cubs were far too useful to be spared. That meant another holiday!

It was frightfully exciting to sit on a mountain of hay, and go jolting across the field. The Cubs took turns at it, but between whiles they worked like slaves. The tramp had lunch with them again, and afterwards he took them to see the barn where he had made himself a fine little camp.

At last the splendid moment came when the Cubs were sitting in a row on the narrow little seats, made of planks, and covered with red baize. They had the top row, and were well raised above people's heads.

Punctually at 2.30 the performance began. There were tight-rope walkers in pink tights and spangles, and performing dogs, and people who rode on white horses standing up, and jumped through paper hoops, and many other things. But of course they liked Buffalo Bill the best, with the Indians and horses and the thrilling noise of revolvers.

One thing disappointed them, and that was that the Indian Jugglers and Famous Dancer did not appear at the afternoon performance. They were to be on that night. The evening show was not till 8 o'clock, and Miss Prince said, "No," when they asked if they might go to it.

CHAPTER XV

A KNIGHT OF KING ARTHUR

And so Danny was alone as he walked across the village green towards the circus field. He was keen to see those jugglers and the marvellous conjurer, for tricks appealed to the detective instinct in him, and he was wonderfully good at discovering how they were done.

The sun had just set, leaving in the sky a red glow that was fading quickly into green. In the soft purple dusk the flaring lights away ahead in the circus field looked very weird. Black figures hurried about, making a confused shouting. The boat swing swayed regularly like the pendulum of a huge clock. And over all there was the monotonous sound of the organ in the roundabout, playing the same tune over and over again.

Danny had the strange feeling in him which said, "Something is going to happen." But what he did not know. Before long he was through the gate, and himself one of the figures moving about between the flaring lights. He could hear now what the shouting was. It was the cocoanut-shy man persuading people to have a shy, while the lady at the toffee-stall tried to shout him down and make them spend their money with her instead.

Many other people were shouting, too, and stalking about in the field Danny noticed Black Bill. He was giving final orders before the performance began. Presently he went up to a big yellow caravan, mounted the steps, and banged on the door. Someone inside opened it—a very ugly old woman.

Black Bill spoke a few words to her, and she brought out someone else, all shrouded up in a big black shawl. Taking this figure rather roughly by the arm, Black Bill led it through the crowd towards the performers' entrance of the big tent. Just then a bell was clanged and clashed, and the crowd began to surge into the performance.

Danny went with it. He had one of the reserved seats in the front row.

It was the same performance as he had seen in the morning, but at last came the time for the troupe of Indian Jugglers. They entered amidst loud applause. There were two jugglers, a conjurer, and the famous dancing girl. They all had dark-brown faces, and were dressed in gorgeous colours, and much gold lace. The jugglers performed first, juggling with plates and balls and knives. Then came the dancer. Danny thought he was going to be rather bored with her, but as soon as she began he was spellbound. He had never before seen anything so quick or active or graceful. And she was cheered and encored again and again, and each time her dance was different. At last she sank down tired out, and Danny had a chance of looking at her face.

The first thing that struck him was that she looked frightened. He saw her glance anxiously at Black Bill. Then it struck him that if she had not been dark brown she would have been very pretty. Then he noticed that she had grey eyes, and he began to feel sure that she was a white girl painted brown. He had just come to these conclusions when the conjurer stepped forward and began his tricks.

Unlike an English conjurer, he had no table, but kept all his things—strange baskets, silk cords, bangles, knives—on the floor. Behind sat the dancing girl on a cushion, and also the jugglers. Presently the conjurer asked for a volunteer to come and help with the trick.

Before any one had time to move Danny was over the

balustrade, and had stepped up and offered his services. He always did this at entertainments, and had been able to discover many a trick by keeping his eyes open. It was a difficult trick; another volunteer was called for, and the two jugglers were also used to hold out a big Turkish rug. When Danny had done what was required of him for the moment he was told to sit down on one of the cushions and wait till he was wanted again. It was as he sat here, not far from the dancing girl, that something began to happen.

While the conjurer talked and the people laughed he heard a voice say in a faint whisper:

"Don't turn your head, Scout, but listen to me."

"Yes?" he said.

"I am being kept prisoner by Black Bill. I am miserable. Oh, rescue me, rescue me!"

"I will—but how?" said Danny, keeping his eyes on the conjurer, and pretending to laugh as if he was amused at his jokes.

"Come to the big yellow caravan at midnight. Knock three times. Black Bill will be out. The old woman sleeps sound. Then we can make a plan."

Danny's heart beat wildly. Here was an adventure such as he loved. And the chivalry of rescuing a maiden in distress made him feel he was like one of Arthur's knights. Then a thought flashed into his mind—the tramp's missing daughter!

As Danny sat in the centre of the circus ring with the gas-lights flaring and the band playing, it all seemed to him like some strange dream, or as if he had stepped back into the past and was part of a fairy tale. And there was a "princess" in the fairy tale, too. The frightened grey eyes of the poor little dancer, with her brown face and gleaming jewels, had awakened a chivalrous sense in him, that said, "I will save her, or die in the attempt!"

Before long the time came for him to step forward and help the conjurer once again—she had whispered her instructions only just in time. Danny cared no longer for the tricks; he scarcely noticed what was happening during the rest of the performance; his mind was working hard, turning over plans by which he could save the girl from the clutches of Black Bill, and get her out of the gipsy camp unseen.

The conjurer having finished all his tricks the Indian troupe went off, and ladies in pink tights came on, riding white horses. But Danny had no eyes for these; through a crack in the canvas he watched Black Bill throw a cloak around the dancer and lead her out.

At last the show was over. The crowd surged out, and Danny with it. In such a crush it would be easy to get near the yellow caravan, unnoticed. Then it struck him that his scout uniform would make him a marked figure. He must look as ordinary as possible, so as to attract no one's attention. Slipping into a dark corner between the big tent and the lion's cage, he began to disguise himself as best he could. Taking off his hat he hid it under a heap of dirty straw. His red neckerchief he folded up and put in his pocket. Taking off his shirt he turned it inside out and put it on again, thus hiding from sight his badges, Leader's stripes, shoulder names, etc. He pulled up his stockings over his knees, and then, as a last bright idea, tied an old piece of sacking round his waist, like an apron. He had noticed that the boy who cleaned out the animals' cages wore just such an apron. Now, by the flickering light of the gas flares, he would pass as one of the circus hands.

Mingling with the crowd, he made his way towards the yellow caravan. It stood a little apart; there was no cover near enough to conceal his approach. What should he do? He stood looking about him. He must hide somewhere, for it was not quite eleven yet; there was over an hour to wait until the coast would be clear for him to go to the yellow caravan. At eleven all the people would be turned out of the circus field, and only the gipsies would be left. Then, to his relief, he noticed that the cart belonging to the boat swings was the nearest one to the yellow caravan. It was empty save for the big tarpaulins used for covering the swings when they were packed up. It would be a perfect hiding place. He waited until some of the crowd moved that way, and then he went too. Climbing quickly up by the wheel he slipped softly inside and drew the tarpaulin over him. Breathlessly he listened, but there was no sound of any one following him.

Presently a clock struck eleven, and a bell, like a very loud muffin bell, clanged above the other circus noises, and Danny listened to the sound of the crowd going out at the gate and making its way homewards along the country roads. Then, very stealthily, he managed to peer out. He saw a crowd of the gipsies collected round the big camp fire. The red glow lit up their faces. Others hurried about, clearing up. And among them Black Bill strode to and fro, giving orders.

Danny had managed to arrange himself in such a way that he could see out quite easily, and yet not be seen. He watched anxiously while the gipsies moved about, and one by one retired to their caravans. At last there was no one left but the two night watchmen by the fire. Black Bill had also retired to his caravan, which was drawn up alongside the yellow one. At about a quarter to twelve Danny saw him come out and walk towards the gate. The two watch men were evidently good scouts, for they both turned at once and watched him go.

"Now's my time," said Danny to himself, with a queer feeling within him, half of excitement, half of fear. The question of how he should cross the open space from his hiding-place to the yellow caravan troubled him, for the two night watchmen might very easily see him. "If only a cloud would pass across the moon, I would make a dash for it," he told himself. Then he noticed something. The moon was throwing the black shadow of the boat swings right across the open space to the caravan. It was a narrow strip of shadow, but a good Scout can make use of the smallest cover.

Slipping softly down from the cart on the side farthest from the watchmen, Danny crawled round and lay quite flat for a moment in the shadow. But the men did not move or turn their heads—they had not heard him. Then, dragging himself along on his elbows, he slipped like a snake along the black line, which made him invisible. When he was half-way across, one of the ponies grazing near started, with a snort of surprise. The two men turned at once and looked straight in Danny's direction. Instantly he dropped his head, hiding his face in the grass; it was the only white thing about him, and might attract their attention. With pounding heart he waited, not moving a muscle. But there was no sound of approaching footsteps. Slowly he raised his head and looked. Thank God, the men had not seen him!

Slowly, slowly he crept on, until he passed under the caravan. At last he was safe on the other side. Standing up on the hub of the wheel he tapped gently on the window. It was opened at once and he found himself face to face with the dancing girl.

CHAPTER XVI

DANNY FINDS MARIETTE—
AND IS KIDNAPPED

She was no longer a dark-brown colour, nor had she long black hair. As Danny looked at her sad little pale face it seemed to him that she was extraordinarily like the Tramp!

"Oh, you've come, you've come—thank God!" whispered the girl. "I knew you would," she added. "Scouts are like the knights in old days, aren't they?"

"Yes," said Danny, "I promised I would. Tell me, quick, what am I to do?"

"Listen," said the girl, "and I'll tell you who I am. We can talk safely, because Black Bill will be out half the night, and old Hannah is in a heavy sleep—she drinks, and once asleep nothing will wake her. First, I must tell you, I'm not a gipsy, like these people———"

"I can see that," said Danny.

"Well, they stole me from my daddy ages ago—I think it must be seven or eight years. They've always kept me shut up in this place, except when they take me out and make me dance. When I used to cry for my daddy Black Bill used to beat me. I don't cry now—I'm too miserable. They never give me a chance to talk to any one. But I read in a paper about Scouts, and when I saw you sitting so close to me at the circus, suddenly a great hope seemed to jump up in my heart. I was sure if you knew how terribly miserable I am you would help me to escape."

"Yes, yes!" said Danny. "But tell me, what was your father?"

"An artist," she said. "Oh, he used to paint such lovely pictures—full of fairies, they were! I often dream of them and—and—of him. Oh, my poor, poor daddy!" she said suddenly, with a great sob. "What have you done all these years without your little Mariette?" A big tear rolled down her cheek.

"I say, don't cry!" said Danny, giving her his handkerchief. "Your daddy is quite near here. He is spending his life hunting for you, and praying God to let him find you. I promised to help him. How good God is to have let me find you!"

"I prayed, too," whispered Mariette.

"Now," said Danny, "how can we get you away? Shall I creep out of the field and fetch a party of police and men and have Black Bill arrested?"

"No, no," said Mariette in a terrified whisper, "don't leave me, don't leave me! Take me with you—take me to my daddy! If you brought police it would be no use. Black Bill has a terrible way of hiding me. Besides, he is friends with all the police. It would be no good. Oh, take me with you!"

Danny looked about him. Would it be safe to take her across the open ground and get through the hedge? He would risk it. Once through they could run, and he knew every gap and short cut. They would make straight for the barn where her father was living during the hay harvest. He would think it was a wonderful dream when he saw his little Mariette, her golden curls shining in the moonlight, as if she really was a moonlight fairy.

"Can you climb out of the window?" whispered Danny.

"Yes," she said. But before she had time even to begin, a cry of horror broke from her, and Danny started violently, for a rough hand had been laid on his shoulder.

"All right, young scoundrel," said Black Bill, as Danny turned round and faced him. "Out of the window? That's your little game, is it? We'll see about that!"

Taking a piece of cord out of his pocket he knotted Danny's wrists behind his back, then tied his feet together. Dragging him round to the caravan door he propped him up against the steps and entered.

A few blows woke old Hannah from her heavy sleep. He could hear Black Bill giving her orders. His struggles to free himself were useless; and even if he could have run away he would not have done so, for his one thought was to stay and help Mariette.

The noise had brought the two watchmen on the scene. They stood there quaking at the thought of what Black Bill would do to them for having allowed a stranger to intrude into the camp. And, sure enough, his rage was terrifying when he came out and saw them. When he had finished abusing them he sent one of them to fetch his two sons. Before long they had arrived. Taking one of them aside Black Bill gave him some instructions in a low voice, and turning to the other told him to loose Danny's feet, blindfold and gag him, and then lead him to the happy home Black Bill had ready for him.

"All right, young scoundrel," said Black Bill. "That's your little game, is it?"

As the dirty handkerchief was tied over his eyes intense rage filled Danny's heart.

"Good-bye, Mariette!" he shouted, before his captor could stop him. "Go on praying—we shall escape all right in the end!" Then a thick muffler was fastened over his mouth, and he felt himself being led away across the grass.

Over rough ground they went, along lanes, across ploughed fields. Every now and then Danny was lifted up and pitched roughly over a gate, or dragged through a hedge. It seemed to him that they had been walking for miles when at last his captor halted, and he heard the sound of a key grating in a rusty lock. He felt himself being led through a doorway, and his feet resounded with a hollow sound as he walked over a wooden floor.

"Sounds like an empty house," he told himself. And the musty, close smell seemed to confirm this idea. Another door was unlocked, and Danny felt himself being led down some stone stairs. Then through another door they passed.

"Loose him," said Black Bill's harsh voice. This was done, then taking up an old tin can, BlackBill's son went out and returned with it full of water. By it he placed a loaf.

"There you are," said Black Bill; "you can feast on that for a few days. It will teach you not to come prying into other people's business. Come," he added, turning to his son. The two men went out, slamming the door behind them, and Danny heard their heavy footsteps going up the stairs.

Gradually his eyes got used to the darkness, and he found he was in a kind of cellar. It was empty save for a heavy wooden settle at one end. The only opening, besides the door by which he had entered, was a little barred window some ten feet up in the wall.

Sitting down on the settle, Danny heaved a heavy sigh. Then he suddenly remembered something, grinned, and began to whistle.

"Well," he said, "this is an adventure anyhow, and I'm sure to come out all right."

CHAPTER XVII

THE CUBS TO THE RESCUE

No Danny! There was consternation at the Hall. Where could he be? The Cubs were wild with grief. While all the grown-ups puzzled their heads over the question, the Cubs went straight to the point and arrived at the correct conclusion by a guess. "That old beast, Black Bill, has stolen him," they said. But the grown-ups said it was absurd, and little boys should not talk nonsense. A careful inquiry began as to where Danny had last been seen, and it was soon proved that he had gone down to the circus for the 8 o'clock performance.

"There you are," said the Cubs, "we told you so—Black Bill's stolen him."

Mr. Beak, the bailiff, and the foreman from the farm were sent down to the gipsy camp to make inquiries as to whether Danny had been seen there the night before; but Black Bill said he had not noticed any Scout at his circus, and it was impossible to gather any information.

The Cubs were in despair.

"Look here!" said David, "we must take the search into our own hands. Let's call a Council." So they called a Council, and the whole Six assembled in the old pigsty.

"Boys!" cried David, standing on an upturned trough, "Danny, our chief, has been stolen by Black Bill. No one will believe it—no one will go to his rescue. Who is ready to take up the quest? Who will promise to die rather than give up the search?"

"I!" yelled everybody, jumping up.

David was very pale; this was no game, and the sorrow and anxiety of the Cubs was very real. "Let us all swear, here, to each other, as Cubs, that we will go out and face any danger, and not rest till we have found Danny."

Solemnly they promised. Suddenly Nipper cried, "P'raps he's dead!" And buried his face in a truss of straw and made noises that sounded suspiciously like sobs. The others turned away in disgust; it's all very well to feel like crying—any chap may do that—but no Cub gives in to himself and does it, he sets to work and does something really useful and helpful.

Bill cleared his throat and began to speak.

"I vote," he said, "that we elect David boss of this show, and make proper plans, and then start off at once."

So a serious Council started. The boys were paired off in twos—David and Hugh (the gamekeeper's son), and Bill and Jack (the blacksmith's son), and, of course, Nipper and little Bobby Brown.

We cannot here recount all that the Council decided, but we will follow each pair, and see what adventures befall them, as they set out, like the knights of old, bent on rescuing their captured chief.

It had been decided that Bill and Jack should go to the camp and reconnoitre. David and Hugh were bent on another quest—but more of that later.

The gipsies were striking camp. Black Bill seemed in a great hurry to get a move on, and was swearing at his men, right and left. Walking along the side of the meadow, by the hedge, Bill and Jack kept their eyes open for any clue that might present itself, and before long they were rewarded.

"Look!" whispered Bill, suddenly gripping his companion's arm, and pointing. "Danny's hat!"

Dropping into cover behind the hedge the two Cubs peered

through at the strange sight before them—a ragged gipsy boy, barefooted, and clad in an old red shirt, wearing a P.L's hat. The boy was busy clearing out the straw from the lion's cage. There was no one near.

"Let's ask him where he got it," said Jack. "We might get some clues from him, and if we could get hold of the hat, it would be a proof that Danny was in the camp, and that something must have happened to him." So the two Cubs stood up, and looked over the hedge at the gipsy boy.

"Where did you get that hat?" asked Bill. He had no intention of making an impertinent remark, but the boy seemed to see something very offensive in the question.

"Nah, then, none o' yer cheek!" he said, and flung a lump of mud straight into Bill's face. Bill was furious, and started forward, his temper fairly up, when Jack called him back to his senses.

"Don't give in to yourself, you ass," he said. "Don't you see it'll spoil the whole game?"

Bill checked himself; but it was a hard struggle.

"I say," said Jack, over the hedge to the boy, "you might be a sport and tell us where you found that hat, because it belongs to a friend of ours, and if you don't tell us where you found it we shall think you stole it from him."

The boy told them to shut up in such a rude way that Bill flushed up again, but he held himself in.

"Look here," said Jack, "if you will give us back our friend's hat, I'll give you this." He held out a fine, new Scout knife. The boy's only reply was to throw an armful of dirty straw over the hedge, and all over the two Cubs.

"Then," cried Jack, "we'll jolly well take it from you!" And, with these words, he leapt lightly over the hedge, followed by Bill, and caught the big gipsy a neat left-hander under the chin. The boy, taken unawares, was sent sprawling, and Bill lost no time in snatching the hat off his head.

A group of gipsies working further on had seen, and now came towards the group.

"Better clear out," said Jack. "We've got our evidence." Jumping over the hedge they quickly made their way back to the Hall.

They found Mr. Ogden and Mr. Beak talking over the question of Danny's disappearance with a policeman. In a few words they told their story.

"H'm," said Mr. Beak, "look's rather strange. They'll have to account, somehow, for Danny's hat being in the possession of one of their boys."

So the policeman and the bailiff and the two Cubs went down to the camp. Black Bill was interviewed once again. This time he sent for his sons, and questioned them before the policeman.

"Oh, yes," said one of them. "I know about that scout. It was like this here. He got in with a queer lot o' folk what come from the town, not the kind o' people as we likes to encourage in our circus. They was so rowdy and disreputable we had to give 'em a warning, and threaten to call in our friend the policeman here. That made 'em wild, and they started smashing up our Hoop-la with the balls off the cocoanut shie. Our lad, in charge of the Hoop-la, had a scuffle with the Scout, who was the ringleader of all the mischief, and he must have got his hat then. We threatened to report the Scout's behaviour up at the Hall. He took fright at that, and so did they all. They started off for the town, and he begged them to take him too; he was afeared to go in so late, and in the state he was in. So they all went off together."

Mr. Beak and the policeman looked very serious.

"I heard about that lot," said the policeman, "but I didn't know as how the Scout had got mixed up with them. Not the kind of companions as Mr. Ogden would like for him."

"Well," said Mr. Beak, "we'd better go and report this information to Mr. Ogden, and see what further steps can be taken."

Then the Cubs stepped forward, with blazing eyes.

"But d'you mean you believe these beastly lies about Danny?" cried Bill.

Mr. Beak shrugged his shoulders. "Well," he said, "what else can I do? Of course it's very sad, but then Danny should keep out of the way of bad company."

Mr. Beak was one of those weak-minded people who always believe everything they are told, and accept the first solution to any problem that comes along, because it is less trouble than finding out the true one.

"But it's all a lie, a lie, a lie!" shouted Bill. Jack was at his elbow. "Shut up, you bandarlog," he whispered, "look at Black Bill."

Bill glanced up and met the eyes of the circus manager fixed upon him in an awful and piercing scowl. He nearly jumped out of his skin, and for a moment stood still like a rabbit mesmerized by a snake, beneath the gaze of those terrible black eyes. In that moment he felt more sure than ever that Black Bill knew where Danny was.

To the Cubs' dismay Mr. Beak reported the story to Mr. Ogden, who seemed inclined to believe it. But something even worse was to happen. Black Bill himself walked down to the Hall that night with the policeman, to make (so he said) a report of the matter himself to Mr. Ogden.

He had a short interview alone with the Squire, and then went away with a horrible grin on his face. Mr. Ogden came out as white as a sheet, and in a towering rage. He ordered the search for Danny to be stopped, and said he had disgraced himself, and could now shift for himself; he washed his hands of such a young scamp.

The Cubs, in despair, set to work with redoubled energy, and that night a strange adventure befell David and Hugh.

CHAPTER XVIII

DETECTIVES

Whilst Bill and Jack had been getting actively to work in search of Danny, David and Hugh had been making plans. Retiring to a particular and secret den of their own, in a pile of logs, they faced the problem in a really logical way. With pencil and notebook, and the quiet determination of true detectives, they reviewed the situation.

"First," said David, "what do we know?... Danny was last seen going to the circus. Then gipsies are people who are often thieves or something. Danny is a detective. If there was anything fishy about those gipsies he would be sure to get on the scent. If Black Bill caught him at it he would be sure to keep him prisoner, so we had better take it that he has been kidnapped by Black Bill. What do we do?"

"Try not to let Black Bill out of our sight," said Hugh. "Follow him everywhere he goes. Try and get as near to him as possible, in case we can overhear him talking about Danny; and keep our eyes open for any clue there might be."

"Yes," said David thoughtfully, "that's just what we must do. But the circus is moving on this afternoon. It's going to Bradmead—that's five miles away."

"Then we must go, too," said Hugh. "We may have to stay away some time, so we must take all we might want with us. And we must be prepared for anything that might happen."

"Yes," agreed David, "let's make a list." He sharpened his pencil and flattened out his notebook.

"Money," said Hugh. "If you haven't got enough money to buy anything you may want, or to pay for railway journeys, or to bribe people with, you're done. I've got £1 5s. saved up in my money-box. I'll take that."

"I've got a sovereign my godfather sent me last week—a late birthday present, because he was at the front when my birthday was on."

"Good," said Hugh. "Then, food. You must have food with you, because you can't be sure of being able to buy it, and you can't carry on if you're starving."

"Cook," said David, "has been crying ever since she found Danny was lost. If she hears we are going to seek for him she'll give us any amount of grub."

"Rope," said Hugh. "We might have to let ourselves down into a pit, or out of a window."

"Yes," said David, writing in his book, "and the pit might be dark, so we might need two electric lights, and some candles and matches."

"We might have to file some bars," said Hugh. "Put down a file."

"We might have to have a fight," said David, "so I think we'll take two of the old daggers out of grandfather's armoury. We shall have to sharpen them, 'cos they're awfully blunt."

His eyes gleamed fiercely.

Hugh nodded. "But after the fight we might want to do first aid, so I think we must have bandages and lint and things."

David wrote in his book.

"And we might be in an awful hurry," continued Hugh. "What about taking Danny's bike? I can ride it if the saddle is put right down, and you can go on the step. We could hide it somewhere near the gipsy camp, in case of need."

"That's a good idea," said David. "And we might want to disguise ourselves. What about you borrowing a set of your sister's clothes? I'll get the false nose we have for acting, and a pair of specs, and grandfather's Inverness cape. No one would recognize us, then."

"You're right," said Hugh. "And I think we'd better have a map—there's that one Danny was teaching us map reading with."

"Yes, yes," said David, "and a compass, in case we get lost in the dark."

Before long they had collected all the things down on their list, and packed them in an old sack and a carpet bag. Concealing them in their den, under the logs, they set out to go down to the camp, and begin their watch on Black Bill, meaning to come back for the things as soon as they saw signs of the circus getting ready to move.

They had not gone far before they met Bill and Jack returning with Danny's hat, and the story of how Black Bill's son had told the bailiff an awful lie about Danny. This convinced David and Hugh more than ever that Black Bill had kidnapped Danny, and they hurried on towards the camp.

Black Bill did not move from the field all the morning; but the Cubs managed to discover from a little gipsy girl that the camp was going to start for Bradmead directly after dinner. Dinner was then nearly ready, as you could tell from the lovely smell that came from the big black pots on the fire.

"Look here," said Hugh to David, "you stay here keeping your eye on Black Bill, and I'll go on to Bradmead on Danny's bike, and take the things and find a secret hiding-place for them. Then I'll come back towards the caravans, which will be on the move by then. If I can't spot you, I'll make the peewit noise and you answer with the owl's."

So the two Cubs parted.

The long line of caravans set out, soon after Hugh had started. It looked like a giant caterpillar of many colours crawling slowly down the white, dusty road. Black Bill was on his big horse, as usual, and it was all David could do to keep him in sight, as he rode backwards and forwards along the line, for David was keeping himself very carefully under cover.

It would never do for the gipsies to know that the Cubs were following them up, for they must have realized that, however much they had managed to hoodwink the bailiff, the police, and the Squire, the Cubs still had very strong suspicions, and were hot on the trail.

The cavalcade had proceeded nearly three miles when David, crawling along at the bottom of a deep ditch, under a hedge, heard the plaintive cry of a peewit, on the field side of his ditch. He answered with the cry of an owl on the wing. The peewit call sounded again three times in quick succession—a recognized signal. Scrambling up the bank David soon discovered his fellow-detective.

"Hullo," whispered Hugh. "I've found their camping site, and a fine hiding-place for us in an old disused water cistern a few fields away. I've stowed everything there, and camouflaged the opening with some dead branches and an old torn rick-cloth."

"Good," whispered David.

And so the two Cubs pressed on, keeping abreast of the circus, but invisible to the gipsies.

CHAPTER XIX

BY THE LIGHT OF A LANTERN

All the rest of the day David and Hugh kept a close watch on Black Bill's every movement.

Towards evening they noticed a boy leading out his big black horse, saddled and bridled.

"He's going out!" said Hugh. "We must follow him. You stay here and keep watch on the camp, and I'll follow him on Danny's bike."

Creeping off to their secret cache, Hugh found the bicycle, and was on the road with it just as Black Bill rode out of the field. It was no easy thing to keep him in sight, and yet keep far enough behind not to attract his attention. However, Hugh managed to do it.

To his surprise he found they had returned to the village. Here Black Bill dismounted and left his horse at the inn. Then he turned in through the big gates of the Hall. At the gates he met the village policeman, and together they walked up the drive.

Black Bill's interview with the Squire we described before.

"That's rum," said Hugh, as Black Bill came out of the study, a nasty grin on his face. "What ever could he want to say to Mr. Ogden?"

In a few words Hugh explained to Bill that he and David would not be in that night, but he did not say where they were, in case Bill should be questioned by the grown-ups. Then, mounting his bicycle, he set out, once again, to follow Black Bill.

It was nearly dark when they arrived back again at the camp. Hugh was frightfully hungry, and was glad to find that David had fetched some food from the old cistern, and their coats, and a few other things. They had supper, and then decided to take it in turns to curl up in the ditch and sleep, one of them keeping watch.

The last of the summer dusk had been swallowed up in darkness, when David, who was taking the first watch, suddenly strained every nerve to hear and see. Yes—it was Black Bill, softly leaving his caravan, and moving towards the gate!

Waking Hugh, David hurriedly put on the haversack containing all the things the detectives might need. Then the two boys crept out after Black Bill, making no sound with their rubber shoes on the grass.

"Notice carefully the way we are going," whispered Hugh, "or we shall never find our way back." For Black Bill was climbing over gates, crossing fields, and following small paths. At length he reached what looked like a deserted and rather ramshackle cowhouse, standing in the corner of a field. The roar of a train told them that they were near the railway, and the glint of red lights far away beyond the trees, told them a station was about half a mile distant.

Stepping up to the shed Black Bill rapped on it a peculiar knock. The door was immediately opened, and he entered. The door was softly shut, again, after him.

"Let's creep round," whispered Hugh, under his breath, "and see if there is a window or anything we can listen through."

They crawled round to the back of the shed, and, to their joy, saw that there was a hole in the wall of the shed, where some boards had slipped. Under this hole chanced to be a big pile of soiled straw and hay. Climbing softly up on this the Cubs crouched down, keeping their heads low.

"It's quite safe to light up," they heard Black Bill say. "No one ever comes this way; there's no fear of being discovered or overheard."

There was the sound of a match being struck and a lantern being lighted. Cautiously the Cubs peered through the hole, and found themselves looking down on two men, seated with their backs to the hole. The man who had opened the door to Black Bill was a sneaking-looking individual, with a foxy face and mean little eyes. By the light of the lantern they could see the eager expression on his face, and the ugly grin on that of Black Bill. Strange shadows danced in the flickering, yellow light, and a feeling of horror came over the Cubs.

CHAPTER XX

A CONSPIRACY OVERHEARD

"Well," said the stranger, "'ave yer fixed it up?"

"Yes," said Black Bill. "Crale, or Ogden as he calls himself now, will be at the cross-roads at 12.30. I had a talk with him this evening."

The Cubs looked at each other. Mr. Ogden? What could it mean? They had come out to find Danny, but apparently they had got on the track of a bigger mystery than they had bargained for.

"We can turn into the wood," said Black Bill, "and have our little talk with him there. I don't reckon that it'll take very long." He grinned, showing a row of cruel-looking teeth.

"How did you get him to agree to come?" said the foxy-faced stranger.

Black Bill laughed. "I told him," he said, "that you and I were the only ones left of the old gang. That we were working hard for our living, now, and we didn't see why he should swank it as a blooming squire, when we helped him make the money he bunked to America with. I said if he refused to meet us, and talk the matter over, I would make known the whole story to the public, and bring disgrace on his name, and show every one that he is not an honest English gentleman, but a forger, who made off with the swag, letting an innocent man suffer imprisonment for him.

"I told him I had a way of making his story known,

without bringing suspicion on myself; and I said now we'd found him again, we weren't going to let him go."

The Cubs, listening with all their ears, could not make head or tail of all this, for they did not know the story the tramp had told Danny. All they knew was that Mr. Ogden, the twin's grandfather, was having a plot made against him—an extraordinary plot they could not understand. It was their duty to save him.

"And what is yer goin' to say to 'im to-night?" asked the man.

"I'm going to tell him that now he's back, and has got plenty of money, we can start the gang again, with me as boss and him as one of the partners—the partner what provides the money! I've drawn up this statement" (and here Black Bill produced a paper), "and I'm going to say if he doesn't sign it, and keep to it, we will make his story known. Then, I'll make him write a big cheque, as a start off!"

The foxy-faced man rubbed his hands together and chuckled.

What could it mean? The Cubs were sorely puzzled. Then Black Bill said something which made them prick up their ears.

"As to that Scout I caught the other night, I made Ogden agree to leave off the search for him. I've got him safe, and, whatever happens, he mustn't escape."

"Well," said the stranger, "strikes me we'd better be getting a move on, if we are to be at the cross-roads before 12.30."

The two men rose, and the Cubs lay flat on the pile of damp hay.

They heard them go out and slam the door; and their footsteps sounded on the cobbled path outside the shed.

"Now," said Hugh, "what on earth are we to do next?"

"I can't understand it all," answered David, "but if grandfather really has something funny about his past, we had better not tell the police about this meeting at the cross-roads. And yet I hate the thought of him meeting Black Bill alone. You don't know what he might do."

"I've got an idea!" said Hugh suddenly. "Let's rush back and get the bike, and get there before them, and go and tell the whole thing to the Tramp. He would be sure to know what to do. And he would come with us and hear what they all say in the wood."

"Good idea!" said David; and, with all haste, the Cubs set out for the place where the bicycle lay concealed.

CHAPTER XXI

THE "WICKED UNCLE" FOUND AT LAST

Black Bill and his accomplice had set out across the field in a direction which Hugh felt sure would bring them out on to the high road. It was, therefore, with all speed that the Cubs scrambled back along the little path, over gates, and through gaps, until they found themselves once again near the gipsy camp. Fetching the bicycle from their hiding-place in the old cistern, they wheeled it quietly across the grass on to the road. After lighting the lamps Hugh mounted, waited for David to be firmly settled on the carrier of the bike, and then began to fairly hog it down the road. Fortunately for him the way lay almost entirely down hill.

The Cubs must have gone nearly a mile when they noticed two black figures walking in the middle of the road, just ahead. Hugh jammed on his brakes and rang his bell loudly. The figures jumped out of the way, and as the bicycle flashed past them, the golden circle from its lamp lit them up. Unmistakably it was Black Bill and the stranger.

"That's good," panted Hugh over his shoulder; "there's still four miles for them to walk to the cross-roads. I don't suppose they're walking more than four miles an hour, and we must be going about fourteen. We shall get there long before they do."

And sure enough the church clock was striking twelve as the Cubs flashed through the little sleeping village and passed the cross-roads.

"I'm jolly glad there's two of us," said David. "I wouldn't like to be on this job alone. It's so beastly dark, and I hate all these plotting people. I wish I was at home in bed."

"Don't give in to yourself," said Hugh. "Let's stick it out. Once we've found the Tramp we shall be all right."

They turned up the little lane that led to the farm. At the gate they got off the bike and propped it up against the fence. Then they crept across the yard to the barn where the tramp slept.

Hugh was carrying the bicycle lamp. Standing just inside the barn, he flashed it round to find the Mysterious Tramp. Yes, there he was, lying on a pile of straw.

Creeping up to him, David shook him gently.

"Hullo," said the Tramp, opening his eyes, and then sitting up. "Who is it?"

"Us," whispered David; "two of the Cubs." Hugh put down the bicycle lamp, and the two boys squatted in its circle of yellow light.

"What on earth brings you two kiddies here?" said the Tramp.

It was very comforting to hear his cheery voice. The Cubs each got hold of one of his hands.

"Oh, sir," said Hugh, "we are in the middle of such an awful adventure."

"And you want to drag me into it?" said the Tramp.

"Yes," said David, "but it won't be long before they meet at the cross-roads. We want to tell you all the story, and then you will know what to do."

"Fire ahead then," said the Tramp.

David quickly told all they had done, seen, and heard.

As he reached the part about the conspiracy in the cowhouse, the Tramp started.

"What," he said, with sudden feverish interest, "a gang of what?"

"Forgers," said David, dwelling with an enjoyable thrill of horror on the word.

"And they want to re-form the gang," said Hugh, "and make Mr. Ogden one of the partners—the one who provides the money."

"And they say if he doesn't promise all they want they will tell everybody all about the past, when (as they say) he was the boss of their gang, and made off to America with all the swag. And they say he wasn't called Ogden in those days—his name was Crale."

"What!" said the Tramp, with a sudden, hard, fierce note in his voice that startled the Cubs, and made them peer through the dim light to try and see his face. "What!" he repeated.

"Crale!" said David.

He little knew what that name called up in the mind of the Mysterious Tramp—sad scenes of eight years ago. In the darkness he seemed to see a long white road, winding between green woods, and on the road he himself, a gay young artist, with a little fair-haired girl holding on to his hand, and jumping about for very joy of being alive, and then a dark, sinister-looking house, with Mr. Crale standing at the gate. "The wicked uncle looks very cross this morning, daddy," would say Mariette; "poor wicked uncle, perhaps he wishes he had a little girl. He must be awful lonely."

And then another scene. The sneering face of Crale, as handcuffs are clipped on to the wrists of the young artist, and he (an innocent man) is arrested as a forger. And then his face again, in the court, giving evidence, and showing the false letters, supposed to be from the artist, making over his little girl to one of the members of his gang.

But David was continuing his story, and the Tramp was

obliged to turn his mind from the sad past to the strange present.

"We were hunting for Danny," continued David, "and we heard this plot by accident. We don't much care what happens, as long as we find Danny. We thought we'd better follow up and hear what Black Bill says to grandfather, because it might give us a clue."

"Yes," said the Tramp eagerly. "Yes, we will go to the wood at once and try and hear what passes."

Danny's fate was far from the Tramp's mind. Here at last he was getting close to that which had occupied all his thoughts for nearly eight years. Here was a chance of learning the whereabouts of his little Mariette and—of revenge.

Extinguishing the lamp the two Cubs and their friend crept down the little lane towards the wood. They did not step out into the open, at the cross-roads, but crawled through a gap into the wood, and made their way silently along a narrow mossy path. The clouds had dispersed, and now the moon shone brightly.

Crouching in the black shadow of a holly bush, the three "detectives" took up their position where they could see the white roads, and the signpost in the moonlight, and also command the wide, fern-fringed path leading down the wood, from the little gate.

They had not been waiting long before two black figures appeared, swinging along the Bradmead road. Reading the signpost, they halted and looked around. Then it was that the tall spare figure of Mr. Ogden stepped forward from the gloom and advanced towards Black Bill.

"It's our old friend Crale right enough," said Black Bill, turning to his companion, "but his beard forms a good disguise. Thought he'd pass for a blooming gent, and a high and mighty squire, he did. Here's your old mate, Bingey," he said, turning to Mr. Ogden.

The squire grunted. "Come into the wood," he growled sullenly, "and then get on with what you've got to say."

Moving with the extreme caution Danny had taught them, the Cubs crawled towards the spot where the three men had gone, followed by the Tramp, until they were close enough to hear every word that passed.

"Well," began Black Bill, "this here is our proposition to you, Mr. Crale." He began to unfold a long plan that it was difficult for the Cubs to understand. When he had explained everything he made his threat of exposing Mr. Ogden's shameful past, unless he would agree to fall in with their scheme.

The Tramp was breathing hard; thoughts raced through his brain. Here he was, close at last to his old enemy, and he would have his revenge at last.

"Make your choice," said Black Bill in a threatening voice. "Sign this paper, and write me a cheque for £1,000, or go back to your swell house and wait for the police to come along to-morrow."

The squire stretched out his hand and took the paper. He fumbled in his waistcoat pocket for a fountain pen. Smoothing the paper out on his knee, he bent over it, trying to read it in the moonlight.

"What's this sentence?" he said, peering closer. "How can I sign what I can't even read?" He ran his finger along a line. Black Bill came near, and bent over the paper to see what it was the squire could not understand. He was altogether off his guard and in a defenceless position. Like a steel spring Mr. Ogden's hands shot out, catching him by the throat, and forcing him down on to the ground. At the same moment another figure sprang up from behind a log and grappled with Bingey.

A cry of horror broke from the Cubs and a muffled exclamation from the Tramp. So his revenge was not to be so easy after all. Ogden might yet escape. But even as he looked, he saw the tide turn. The squire, for all his wiry strength and all his knowledge of jujitsu, was a poor match for Black Bill's powerful muscles. Besides, he was well over fifty, and Black Bill was some years younger. The Tramp breathed hard. He was seeing a terrible revenge upon his enemy.

Then, like a golden flash, a memory came into his mind—his conversation with Danny last autumn: "God won't answer your prayers till you forgive your enemies," Danny had said. Revenge was a terrible sin—the Tramp knew that. And then, in those breathless moments he knew that his time for deciding had come. For God's sake he would forgive his enemy. More, he would risk his life to save him. Springing forward he threw himself on to the struggling men.

With a yell of rage Black Bill let go of the squire, and turning on his new assailant aimed a blow at him with a knife. It sank deep into the Tramp's arm, and things would have gone badly for him had not David and Hugh joined into the fray.

Catching hold of Black Bill's legs, they little by little managed to wind them up with the rope they had brought with them. Then, while the squire and the Tramp held him down, they bound his arms also. At last he was helpless, and the Tramp and Mr. Ogden stood up; Bingey had been settled by Mr. Ogden's man, and lay gagged and bound.

CHAPTER XXII

AT DAWN

The Tramp's arm was bleeding badly, and the Cubs' first thought was to bind it up for him with the bandages they had so thoughtfully included in their list of requirements. This done, the party stood looking at each other in silence.

"You have saved my life," said Mr. Ogden, stretching out his hand and speaking in a voice shaken with emotion. "No words can express the gratitude of one man to another who has done that?"

The Tramp smiled a little grimly, and took the outstretched hand. To him this was a handshake of forgiveness.

"I don't know who you are," said the Squire, "but if there is any way in which I can serve you, you will be doing me a favour by letting me know of it."

There was a strange silence. Then the Tramp gave a dry little laugh. "You ruined my life, Crale, eight years ago," he said. "I doubt if you can make up for that now."

The Squire started and reeled back against a tree.

"Graham?" he said. "You?" He peered at him through the moonlight. Then covered his face with his hands.

After a moment he looked up again. "The thought of you," he said, "has haunted me all these years. But I had not the courage to do the only thing that could put things right—give myself up. You have had the courage to save my life and the grace to forgive me. Now, by God's help, your every wrong shall be righted; justice shall be satisfied. What is the use of speaking of this here? Let us get these men back to the Hall. In the morning we will send for the police for their arrest—and mine."

The Cubs were altogether mystified at what was passing. The leading back of Black Bill and Bingey, and their imprisonment at the Hall, filled them with delight. To-morrow morning Danny would be found.

Creeping up very softly the two Cubs made their way to the twin's bedroom. David was soon in bed and Hugh curled up on the sofa. Before long they were asleep.

Meanwhile, in the Squire's study a strange conversation was going on between Mr. Ogden and the Mysterious Tramp.

"Of course I could escape if I liked," said Mr. Ogden, "and just leave everything. But I can't do it now, I can't do it! You've taught me honour and courage and showed me that a more noble spirit is worth while."

"You must thank your Scout Danny for that," said the Tramp. "I was waiting to reap my revenge. It was the thought of him made me do what I did."

"Well," said Ogden, "you've lost all, and suffered for seven years in prison. Justice can never be truly satisfied. But I will do my best to satisfy it. I shall give myself up and plead guilty. I shall suffer seven years in prison—more perhaps. And all this wealth that I made at your expense, sir, will be yours. You will be master of this house, this land, and of my income. As to my grandsons, I leave it to your mercy what you will do with them."

The Tramp gasped with surprise.

"Don't say a word," continued Ogden in a broken voice. "It is all a man can do who truly repents. To-morrow all will be settled with my lawyers."

There was silence. Then the Tramp suddenly stood up. "Money, land, honour—what is this?" he cried. "I don't want this. Give me back the one treasure of my life—my little Mariette!"

Ogden started. "I had forgotten the child," he said. "Of course—of course. Black Bill took her—to-morrow he shall tell what he did with her. And Danny—he kidnapped him, for some reason. He will have to make known where the boy is."

CHAPTER XXIII

"WHAT'S UP?"

"What on earth can be up?" thought Nipper to himself, as he sat up in bed, in the big sunny room that was the three boys' bedroom. There was Hugh asleep on the sofa in his clothes. And there was David (who was to have been out all night) lying in bed, in a wild, restless attitude, one arm flung across the pillow. His hands and face were very dirty, and there was what looked like a smudge of blood across his cheek. His clothes, covered with dust and earth and bits of bracken, lay in a heap on the floor.

Nipper looked about for something convenient to throw at his brother in order to waken him and inquire what was up, but before he had time to do so, something else had attracted his attention. Strolling down the rose walk outside the window, and dipping his head every now and then to avoid the long thorny arm of a rose tree stretched out to hook passers-by, or a dew-drenched branch of crimson rambler, came the Mysterious Tramp. His arm was in a sling, and the sling was made of a Cub's neckerchief. He had a strange look on his face, as if he was puzzled and worried, but also happy.

What could be up? Nipper was about to shout "Hullo" out of the window, when once more his attention was diverted. Running across the field came Bobby Brown.

Of course—he had forgotten—he and Bobby had arranged to meet at seven, and go out in search of Danny.

It must be seven, and he had forgotten to get up quick, and dress. He leaned out of the window to see if it really was seven, by the sundial—he could tell the time by the sundial, it was so much easier than the nursery clock, with its silly gold face and little niggly hands. Yes, the sun said it was six, that meant seven by summer time.

Signing to Bob to wait, Nipper slipped softly out of bed. He decided, after all, not to wake the twins and Hugh; they might go and spoil his adventure. He had a very small pretence at a wash, dressed, had a try to put the comb through his hair, and gave up the attempt, decided not to wash his teeth, knelt down and said his prayers, which were nearly all for the intention of finding Danny, and then slipped gently down the wide oak staircase, and out of a window, into the sunny garden.

He found Bobby Brown standing in the middle of a geranium border, his mouth wide open, and his blue eyes very round.

"Hullo!" said Nipper. "What are you doing—staring at nothing like a stuck pig."

"Sh-sh-sh!" said Bobby, and pointed up at the store-room window a few feet above his head.

"He must be potty," Nipper told himself, and also leapt into the middle of the geranium bed; he had never thought of doing this before; it was delightful to think how angry Mr. Pooks would be if he could see, but it was Bobby who had started it, and Bobby never set bad examples—Miss Prince said so.

"Listen," said Bobby.

Nipper listened. A hoarse, strange voice was talking in the store-room.

The store-room was a small room opening out of the hall. It was always kept locked, because Mr. Ogden kept his guns and fishing rods in there. The windows were barred. Who on earth could be talking in it?

"Make a back, you fat-head, instead of standing there staring, and I'll have a squint," commanded Nipper.

Bobby meekly obeyed, and presented a small fat back, upon which Nipper ruthlessly stepped, with hard and painful boots.

"Ow-w-w-oo!" said Bobby.

"Don't give in to yourself!" replied Nipper, sternly, getting a firmer foothold, and clutching the edge of the window with his fingers. And then he suddenly stood quite still, as if frozen with horror—for he found himself looking full into the face of Black Bill, the one person in the world of whom he had a real dread. And it was Black Bill, with rumpled hair, bits of bracken in his beard, his shirt all torn open at the neck, and hanging in shreds, his arms tied down to his sides, and a look of sullen rage in his terrible eyes.

With a gasp Nipper staggered off Bobby's back and broke five geraniums in his fall. In a few horrified words he explained what he had seen.

"Whatever can be up?" said Bobby.

"That's what I keep thinking," said Nipper. "It's awful mysterious. But we'd better go and search for Danny."

Creeping round to the old cucumber frame where they had hidden their secret store, they drew forth their provisions for the day, and the other things they had collected, as likely to be useful on the expedition for the relief of Danny.

Having packed everything into a small Gladstone bag, they set forth upon their quest, taking turns with the bag, which they carried over their shoulders slung on a stick.

Their methods were as follows: Tramping round the country, they visited every place that they themselves would have chosen as the best place to hide a kidnapped boy in, and walking round it, they shouted as loud as possible a certain call which Danny had taught them, and which it was an understood thing in the Pack must always be answered, whenever and wherever heard.

It was like a huge game of hide-and-seek.

The day before, Nipper and Bobby had visited, among other places, a windmill, seven farms, five churches, four sheds or cowhouses in fields, a boat house, a village football pavilion, the golf club, some waterworks, a lime kiln, and a disused sandpit. But only echoes had answered their oft-repeated call.

Footsore, and sore of throat, and very tired of the Gladstone bag, they had returned home at night, still entirely determined to persevere in the search until they should find Danny. "We won't give in to ourselves," they told each other, every time things were very disappointing, and Danny did not prove to be in the farm buildings, or imprisoned with the golf clubs, or in the coal-holes of the various churches.

We will now leave these two dauntless tenderpads, making their way towards a deserted grange four miles away, and return to what was happening at the Hall.

CHAPTER XXIV

BLACK BILL IS QUESTIONED

The next to wake was Bill. He also wondered what was up, and waking David, made inquiries. It was jolly hard to make head or tail of his twin's story, and Bill wondered if he was by accident telling his dream, instead of yesterday's adventure. But as Hugh seemed to have had the same dream, this could not be the case.

Dressing quickly the boys decided to go down and look for the Mysterious Tramp, who had promised Mr. Ogden that he would remain at the Hall. Walking noiselessly on the thick carpet which covered the stairs, the boys heard Mr. Ogden's voice in the hall, and stopped.

"The old chap's up early," said Bill. "It is only just eight. I wonder what's up."

"Hullo, hullo! Is that 846?" said Mr. Ogden's voice.

"He's 'phoning," whispered David.

"Hullo! Will you please take an important message for Inspector Grey?"

A long message followed, all about Inspector Grey coming himself as soon as possible, with some constables.

Then Mr. Ogden retired to his study and locked the door.

The Cubs found the Mysterious Tramp on the terrace, having a very serious pow-wow with Miss Prince. He stayed to breakfast with them, but was very silent, and not a bit funny—which was disappointing.

"When are you going to make Black Bill say where Danny is?" asked David.

"If he won't say, will you use torture?" inquired Bill the practical.

"Yes, yes!" burst in David, the imaginative; "you could make a lovely thumb-screw with my fretwork vice. But I think slow roasting would be best. If you lit the stove in the billiard-room you could make him sit on it till it got hotter and hotter and hotter, like——"

"No," said the Tramp thoughtfully, looking reprovingly at Miss Prince, who was apparently choking over her buttered toast, "I don't think we shall need to use torture. Black Bill will find it best to plead guilty of everything, and clear up all the mysteries."

"D'you s'pose he's fool enough to tell the truth?" asked Bill. "I tell you it'll have to be torture."

It was soon after breakfast that a long, grey car arrived, bringing the Inspector, a wiry little man in plain clothes and two constables. It was closely followed by a closed car, containing two more constables.

"What a lot of coppers they want to settle two gipsies," remarked Hugh. "My father can deal with three poachers, single-handed."

The first thing that took place was the cross-questioning of Black Bill. As the Tramp had said, he didn't try to justify himself. He said Danny had been prying into his private concerns, and he owned up that he had kidnapped him. He explained exactly where he might be found—namely, in the disused water-mill. He only hoped he had not tried to escape out of the window, and fallen into the river, and got sucked under the wheel.

An expedition hurried off to the mill, to return an hour after with the sad news that Danny was not in the mill, but that there were signs of the room having been recently occupied, and the window overlooking the river being open.

Next came a question asked by Mr. Ogden, while the Tramp listened, holding his breath, a look of intense expectation in his eyes.

"The little gell? Oh, poor little Mariette," said Black Bill. "I'm sorry to say she died soon after Mr. Crale handed her over to me. Fretting for her father must have did it. I know I took good enough care of her, and my old woman tended her as if she had been her own kid."

The Tramp seemed to crumple up. He took no more interest in the rest of the proceedings. He would have gone out, but Mr. Ogden asked him to remain.

When, at last, the business was over, two constables led the gipsies away to the waiting car. Mr. Ogden was accompanied to his study by a policeman, who remained with him, and the Inspector went away in his car.

The Tramp strode quickly out across the garden. As he passed the terrace Miss Prince jumped up as if to ask a question.

"She's dead," said the Tramp, in a cold, dry voice, and walked quickly on.

"Why," said David, later, "is Miss Prince crying on the terrace?"

"Don't ask me," said Bill. "I can't stand crying women."

CHAPTER XXV

THE RESCUE OF DANNY

"The deserted Grange." The very words thrilled Nipper to the marrow. It was Bobby Brown who suggested going there. He knew about it because, once, when out with his father as he drove on his rounds in his dog-cart, Dr. Brown had pointed it out.

It was a smallish, grey stone house, in a straggling garden where a huge army of weeds had nearly choked the flowers, a few of which still fought for existence—a rose or two, and a few thin, sad wallflowers.

A moat ran half-way round the deserted Grange. In one place the walls went right down into the water.

With all the strength of their lungs the Cubs' shouted the familiar call, "Ya-hoo-oo-wah!" and then stood still and listened.

"Ya-hoo-oo-wah! Yah-hoo-oo-wah!" came back a faint answer from the grey walls of the Grange.

"A beastly echo again," said Nipper, in despair. But Billy Brown was clutching his arm with perspiring fingers.

"No, no, Nipper!" he panted; "not an echo; echoes don't say it twice!"

"No they don't!" cried Nipper excitedly. "Bob, you aren't such a chump as I thought you were!"

"Danny—Danny!" shouted Nipper.

"Hul-lo!" came Danny's voice, very faint and far away.

Running through the tangled garden, the Cubs entered the Grange through the open door. Their footsteps sounded hollow and uncanny on the wooden floors. Again they called, and again Danny answered. This time his voice came from below their feet.

"He's in the dungeons!" said Nipper, dwelling on the word with delicious horror. "I expect he's chained up among the skeletons of the men what's been starved to death—like that guide told us at the Castle. It's a good thing there aren't any bloodhounds nowadays."

But try as they would, the Cubs could not force open a single one of the heavy doors that seemed as if they might lead down to the cellar.

"Come round to the window," called Danny. "If you could give me a rope, and break the bars, I could climb up and get out."

The Cubs ran out again into the garden. Before long they had espied what must be the grating of the dungeon—a small, barred window. But, alas! it was in the wall which went down into the moat. Calling out once more, they found Danny's voice certainly came from this window. What should they do?

Then the puzzle was suddenly solved, for, moored to a stump they discovered an old and rotten punt. It was half-full of water, but this did not matter. Getting in, they pushed off from the bank with two long sticks, and punted themselves across.

"Here we are!" they said, as they reached the barred window.

"Thank God!" came Danny's voice. "I knew He wouldn't let me die here!"

"What shall we do?" said Nipper.

"Let down a rope; about five foot would do," said Danny.

The Cubs looked around them in despair. They hadn't got a rope. Then Nipper caught sight of the chain by which the punt had been moored to the bank. This the Cubs let down through the grating, and then hung on to it for dear life. Soon Danny's face appeared at the window. It filled them with horror, for he looked years older and as pale as a ghost, with grey shadows under his eyes.

"Oh, how ripping to see you kids!" he said. "You don't know all I've suffered in that damp hole, with the rats, and no food."

The bars were thin and rusty, but Danny could not manage to break them. Punting themselves back to the other side of the moat, the Cubs collected two enormous stones, and then punted back.

Danny slipped to the ground again, and by dint of a few tremendous blows with the stones, the Cubs smashed in the bars. Letting down the chain, they then hauled Danny up once more. Crawling through the tiny window he stepped into the punt.

"Quick—she's sinking!" he said, and got her back to the bank only just in time.

"Now," said Danny, "for home, and then to rescue Mariette!"

CHAPTER XXVI

WHERE'S THE TRAMP?

As Danny and the two Cubs stood together on the mossy bank of the moat, the old punt sank.

"She did a good bit of work on her last voyage," said Nipper, as if he was speaking of a first-class cruiser, or a mine-sweeper at least.

"I wonder she kept up as long as she did," said Danny, "she'd got a huge hole in her bottom. I got a horrid shock when I saw what you two kids were in."

"But it wouldn't have mattered if she had sunk," said Bob, "you had taught us both to swim. Don't you remember what a job you had with Nipper—he would play about all the time, and splash everybody, instead of practising? I always did my best all the time, and didn't give in to myself."

Nipper hurriedly changed the subject.

"You must be awfully hungry," he said to Danny, "or did you eat rats? Look, we've brought you a lot of grub. Sit down and eat it before we start home—there's four miles to walk."

Danny shuddered. "No, I didn't eat the rats," he said. He sat down on the bank, and made short work of all the grub the Gladstone bag contained.

"That's better," he said at last. He looked an absolute scarecrow, his shirt still inside out, no neckerchief, and smears of dirt all over his very pale and haggard face.

They were only able to go slowly, for Danny ached from head to foot, for the place had been terribly damp, and the rats had prevented him from sleeping a wink.

"Did you give up hope?" said Nipper.

"No," replied Danny. "A Scout never gives up hope. But it was pretty ghastly. My only comfort was in thinking that I was suffering like Sir Thomas More in the Tower of London, and the martyrs who were shut up in 'Little Ease'—the rats used to swim into it at high tide, you know."

They had got to the road by now, and Danny's heart sank at the thought of a four mile walk; but he said nothing.

However, his good angel had not deserted him yet. They had not walked a hundred yards before a farm cart passed them, piled high with a load of straw. In the country everybody gives anybody a lift, and the friendly carter nodded his assent to Nipper's request.

Danny and the Cubs clambered up, and were soon curled up in a comfortable nest. Then Danny told them the whole story, and they told him the extraordinary things they had discovered that morning.

The cart dropped the little party at the gates of the Hall, and they walked up the long drive. Arrived near the house, Nipper and Bob began to swell with pride. They, alone, of all the search parties had been successful! They had rescued the hero of the story! Each taking one of Danny's hands, they led him in triumph on to the terrace, where a little crowd of people were sadly discussing Danny's fate.

A cheer went up from the four other Cubs, who threw themselves on Danny like so many wild animals. The bailiff and the policeman crowded round. The cook came rushing out of the kitchen, her eyes still red, and laughed and wept, for joy, and kissed Nipper and Bobby (much to their

disgust), and promised to make them cream meringues and ices and jam puffs, and "hanythink helse they liked to hask for, bless their little 'earts."

Danny strove to get out of the excited mob. "I'll tell you all about it soon," he said, "but there's one person I must see before I do anything else—I must see the Tramp—I've got something very important to tell him, and no time must be lost."

"Where's the Tramp?" everybody asked everybody else. No one knew. So the whole party scattered, to hunt. Miss Prince tried to persuade Danny to stay and rest. "The poor Tramp," she said, "has had a terrible blow. I'm afraid it's broken his heart. He strode off, early this morning, and I should say he's gone off to walk miles and miles, to be alone with his grief."

But nothing would restrain Danny—he insisted on going just as he was to search. He walked off through the wood, past the very spot where, last year, the Mysterious Tramp had come walking down the mossy path, and into their lives. What strange things had happened since then! After all, St. Antony, "the saint who finds lost things," and whose statue had seemed to the Tramp to be pointing out that mossy path to him from his niche in the little grey church at the cross roads, had found the little lost girl!

Danny passed the gamekeeper's cottage, and recalled that sad conversation in the early morning sunlight, when the Tramp had spoken of his quest of revenge, and Danny had told him it was not much use to expect to get his prayers heard, when he kept revenge in his heart.

"He must have forgiven his enemies," Danny told himself, "and that was why God answered his prayer." He walked on through the wood, and climbed the fence on to the road.

The church door stood wide open, as usual, and Danny crossed the road to turn in and say thank you for having been rescued from death, and for the finding of Mariette.

The church was very dim and quiet—full of a holy feeling. A golden ray of sunlight fell across the sanctuary. Danny knelt down reverently. At first he thought he was alone. Then he saw a dark figure, bowed down on the step, before the altar; and suddenly a strained, hoarse voice broke through the silence: "O God, this is too much, too much. I lived in the one hope that You were merciful, that You would give her back to me at last: and all the time she was dead, dead, dead. And yet … if it's Your Will … I accept it...."

Danny got softly up and slipped out of the church. It is wrong to listen to any one speaking to another—but most of all to someone speaking alone to God. He sat down on a tree-stump in the churchyard, and waited. Presently a step made him glance up. The Mysterious Tramp stood framed in the archway of the porch, the sunlight falling on his thin, sad face. But there was a strange look of peace and steadfastness in his eyes that Danny had never seen there before.

He walked down the path and would have passed by had

not Danny got up. Stepping up to the Tramp he took his arm.

"I say," he said, "we must thank God for something. I've found your little Mariette."

The Tramp reeled back, and then stood gazing at Danny in silence.

"What do you mean?" he said at last. "Found my little Mariette? But she's dead—dead!"

"No," said Danny, "she's alive, and in a yellow caravan, longing and longing for her daddy. I was just rescuing her, like King Arthur's knights rescuing a maiden in distress, when Black Bill took me prisoner and very nearly made an end of me."

As they walked back together through the wood, Danny told the Tramp the whole story of the finding of Mariette. He longed to inquire about the capture of Black Bill, and all the other strange happenings, but he could see that the Tramp could think of nothing but his little girl.

CHAPTER XXVII

THE FINDING OF MARIETTE

Inspector Grey's car once more hummed along the dusty road, but this time it contained, besides the two constables, Danny and the Mysterious Tramp.

The gipsy camp was still at Bradmead, but the swings were all folded up, the big tent was down, there was no monotonous music from the merry-go-round. The whole camp was under arrest. Black Bill's sons and all the men-folk had been taken into custody. Six stalwart policemen were on guard, keeping an eye on the women and children.

Going up to the yellow caravan, Inspector Grey beat a sharp rat-tat on the door. A hideous old woman put out her head and said: "Whaat-cher waant?" But when she saw the police she became polite and whiny-piny. Inspector Grey ordered her to get out of the caravan. She wouldn't at first, and said: "It wasn't no place fit for a nice gentleman like him to go in." So the stalwart policeman chivalrously handed her out and the Inspector entered.

Presently he reappeared at the top of the steps, holding by the hand a pale little girl in a tattered brown dress and a shock of uncombed golden hair.

A cry of joy broke from the Tramp.

"Mariette!"

He stood with open arms at the bottom of the yellow steps.

For a moment she looked at him with wide grey eyes. Then recognition began to dawn in them. "It's—my—daddy!" she cried, and jumped down into his arms.

Inspector Grey looked the other way, and the policeman blew his nose—he was a family man himself.

The morning sun filled the big library, and shone on the musty old leather-backed books, the mahogany table, and quaint dog-irons in the fireplace.

Very silent and wide-eyed, David, Bill and Nipper sat on three big leather chairs. The Mysterious Tramp (now clad in a grey flannel suit, his arm in a black silk sling) sat in a deep armchair; and on the hearthrug stood Mr. Ogden, his face set and pale, his knobbly hands working nervously.

"Boys," he said, "my grandsons; Mr. Graham—I have something to say to you of a very grave nature. It is difficult to say—let us get it over quickly.

"In the past I was guilty of a very terrible crime. To cover my own guilt and to escape its just punishment, I played a horrible trick upon an innocent man, by which he was accused of my crime. He suffered the seven years' imprisonment that was my desert. He lost the little daughter whom he loved. He lost all. His career was ruined. He was turned out into the world—a tramp.

"And I? I lived here in luxury—luxury bought at his expense. Did my luxury make me happy? No. The canker of remorse was eating into my heart.

"Then came a memorable night when the man I had wronged saw me in the power of my enemies, saw his wrong about to be avenged. But he had forgiven me. He did that which is the highest sign of love which one man can give another—he risked his life to save mine.

"What can I do to repay him for all he has unjustly suffered? I can only give him all I have—this house, my wealth. You, my grandsons, I have entrusted to his care. He is your guardian. Obey him as if he was your father. And what is to happen to me? Many years of prison are due to me. I cannot look any man in the face until I have paid my debt to justice.

"To-day I go to London to await my trial. I shall go to prison. If I ever come out alive I shall have to depend on the charity of the man I have wronged. Good-bye, my children, good-bye. Remember what I have told you. If you ever sin against man and against God confess your sin and bear your punishment, or life will hold only bitterness for you, and death only fear. Pray for me sometimes, and be good sons to this man."

Very stiffly, he gave each boy a kiss, shook hands with the Tramp and, turning, strode out of the room.

There was a whir and buzz, and Inspector Grey's car moved away down the drive.

Luncheon was a rather silent meal. Mariette did most of the talking; and there was one fairly animated argument between her and Nipper, as to which end you should cut a cucumber.

"Look here, we really must cheer up," said the Tramp, as they rose from the table and walked out into the hall. "Well, kiddies, what do you think of your new father?"

"We are jolly glad!" said Bill. "Shall we call you Father?"

"You sha'n't call him Daddy," said Mariette quickly.

"Yes, you can call me Father, if you like," said the Tramp, laughing.

"And we've got a sister, now!" said David.

"Yes," said Mariette shyly. She had a marked preference for David, who protected her from Nipper.

"And Danny can be our big brother," said Bill, who hadn't much use for girls.

"All we want now," said Nipper, "is a mother." Then a bright idea struck him. "Miss Prince can be our mother!" he cried.

Danny kicked him, and told him in a whisper to shut up, but Nipper didn't see why he should shut up over such a splendid idea.

"But she can be our mother, can't she?" he said, appealing to the Tramp.

"Yes, yes!" cried the others altogether—even Mariette, who had already found in Miss Prince the mother's tenderness she had never known.

"Can she be our mother? Say yes, say yes!" pleaded Nipper, clinging to the Tramp's hand.

"Don't be so previous, Nipper," said the Tramp. "I was only waiting for all you chaps to clear out, to ask Miss Prince that myself. Come," he said, stretching out his free hand towards her, "let's go out into the garden and hide our blushes—this is too painful!"

As they went out of the French window Nipper caught hold of Miss Prince's hand.

"Say yes," he whispered—"to please me."

"All right," whispered back Miss Prince.

And that is how the three naughty boys at the Hall became three good boys, and obtained a father, a mother, a sister, and best of all, a big brother—Danny, the Detective.

THE END.

9 789355 175830